THE LOVING GOD

Wilfrid J. Harrington OP

The Loving God

the columba press

First published in 2012 by
the columba press
55A Spruce Avenue, Stillorgan Industrial Park,
Blackrock, Co Dublin

Cover by Bill Bolger
Origination by The Columba Press
Printed in Ireland by Gemini International Ltd

ISBN 978 1 85607 744 6

Contents

Preface

'I believe in one God, the Father, the Almighty.' We Christians solemnly profess our faith in God. One may ask: Who is this God of our faith profession? I have become increasingly conscious of the absolute importance of our image of God – how we perceive God. It is important for our response to God and for the manner in which we live out our response. It is critical for anyone with pastoral concern. Over the years I have written of God – the God revealed in the Old Testament and the God revealed in and by Jesus Christ. I have discerned a striking consistency in the revelation and have perceived a wondrously attractive and deeply comforting portrait of our God.

Here, together with fresh insights, I draw on aspects of those studies. My hope is to display something of the God who is the *Abba* of Jesus – and our *Abba* too. All I claim is that this is the God I discover in the Bible. This is the God in whom I believe – the God of my hope. Paul reminds us that 'Now we see in a mirror dimly, but then we will see face to face' (1 Corinthians 13: 12). We may, here and now, glimpse the true God and be comforted and sustained. We can be sure that the gracious God who will welcome us home is a loving God wholly beyond our fondest imagining.

Wilfrid J. Harrington OP

Introduction

'Long ago God spoke to our ancestors in many and various ways by the prophets, but in these last days he has spoken to us by a Son' (Hebrews 1:1-2). Here we shall focus on that revelation to our ancestors – on the Old Testament. The reason is because, for many, the God of the Old Testament is a forbidding figure. It is a misconception that cries out for challenge. It will be shown that God is gracious and loving and displays unyielding concern for us.

Any consideration of God must, first of all, face the fact that what we may know of God is only what limited human intelligence can fathom. God, strictly speaking, is Mystery. We acknowledge that the God of our faith is Creator, Source and Sustainer of all that is, a Creator who maintains a loving relationship with his creation. Our God desires dialogue with his human creatures. In furthering his plan of salvation for sinful humanity, he chose and called one human family to be his special people, to bear witness to him. The call was marked by promise and was sealed by covenant. When this people proved unfaithful, their God remained constant and faithful.

Traditionally, God has been cast as a just Judge. Consideration of the biblical notion of justice will suggest that this role be re-examined. And, in place of a 'wrathful' God, we should look to a suffering God. There can be no questioning the mercy of God. What must be questioned is *our* tendency to limit its range. God, indeed, had resolved to bear with an obdurate people. At their best, that people, in prayer of lament and repentance, showed their appreciation of God's forbearance. They were prepared to believe that God would show mercy to the whole of humankind. The author of the first Letter of John has proclaimed with eloquent directness: 'God is love' (1 John 4:7, 16). The God of love is manifest in the scripture of Israel. He is the gracious God, alert to human suffering, forgiving of human sin.

'In these last days he has spoken to us by a Son.' God has spoken his definitive word – the Word-made-flesh. Jesus of Nazareth is Immanuel – God-with-us. He is the one who has defined God. The God of his definition is the only true God. This Father of our Lord Jesus Christ is found in the Old Testament – by those who have eyes to see.

In the Preface I observed that I look back on a pondering, over several years, on the God of the Bible. A list of the relevant writings can be found in the Notes section at the end of this book.[1]

CHAPTER ONE

Holy Mystery

I am God, and there is no other;
I am God, and there is no one like me …
(Isaiah 46:9)

'I believe in God.' We confidently make our profession of faith. But, do we pause to think what we might mean by 'God'? We are ever tempted to construct a God in our image. And we have attempted to manipulate God. People may have gods in their lives – they may not recognise them as such, but they worship them. More serious are false images of the true God. God deserves better than the insult of ungracious caricature. It might be argued that the more insidious enemy of God is not atheism but religion. Most atheists reject not God but the travesty-God presented by religion and by the conduct of those who profess to worship God.

Modern Theism

A pervasive vision of God in our day is that of a monarch who dwells on high, rules the world and judges human conduct. 'He' is the most powerful individual in the whole of reality. This Supreme Being is the target of modern atheism. Challenge to, and rejection of, this 'God' are in fact justified. This 'God' is a product of the eighteenth-nineteenth century European movement known as the Enlightenment. It maintained that the world is to be understood through the 'enlightened' medium of human reason and not in light of dogmatic religious authority. In counter-attack, Christian theologians adopted the philosophical approach of their opponents. They used rational arguments to defend the existence of God.

Starting with the natural world, they reasoned to the existence of God using a process of inference, thereby constructing a theology where God appears as the highest component in the intellectual system. This all but assured that while God is a powerful individual above other powers in the world, he remains a member of the larger household of reality. His attributes are deduced by a reasoning process that contrasts what is infinite with the limitations of the finite. Thus, God is immutable (only creatures change), incorporeal (bodies are the site of change), impassible (only creatures suffer), omnipotent, omniscient, omnipresent, in contrast to creatures who are limited in power, knowledge and presence.[1]

The resulting view of God, termed 'modern theism', compromises both the transcendence and the immanence of God. Transcendence means otherness beyond all imagination. This is lost when claims about the divine are made answerable to rational argument. Immanence means the nearness of God beyond all imagination. This is lost because that remote monarchic aspect of the divine allows little room for indwelling presence. When filtered through preaching and accommodated in personal piety, this construct of God produces a trivial image of God, unworthy of belief. It is true that, in reply to surveys, most people acknowledge that they believe in God. If pressed, many would admit that their God is an aloof and distant figure. He seems to have no impact on – and little interest in – his creation. For that matter, this concept of God goes hand in hand with a view of creation that regards it as a single moment: God created, and withdrew – an absentee monarch. It is evident that a perception of God as distant and aloof makes it difficult, if not impossible, to have a close relationship with God. At best one might cling to a belief in the existence of a Creator. There is lack of the living faith in a Presence that might be motivation and sustenance. 'You shall love the Lord your God.' My God must be lovable. Otherwise the God I worship is not the true God who loves me beyond measure for myself and as myself. And my life is immeasurably poorer.

Paradoxically, we can begin to speak meaningfully of God only when we acknowledge that God is literally incomprehensible, that the reality of the living God is a mystery beyond all telling. The truth is: much of our God-talk is ultimately meaningless – simply because God is beyond our understanding.

Aquinas has bluntly declared:

> Since our mind is not proportionate to the divine substance,
> God remains beyond our intellect and so is unknown to us.
> *Hence the supreme knowledge that we have of God is to know that*
> *we do not know God* insofar as we know that what God is sur-
> passes all that we can understand.[2]

Holy Mystery

God is Mystery, wholly different from anything we know in our
world. The human mind, in short, can shape no adequate idea of
God. Consequently, no human word about God can be taken literally. We speak of God analogically. One makes an affirmation:
God is good. This must be immediately qualified: God is not
good in the manner of creatures. The conclusion: God is Source
of all good. But, what is Source of all good? In fact, our human
understanding of God gives us but the faintest inkling of Good
that is Source of goodness. Similarly, our human understanding
of love, even at its finest, can give us no real appreciation of divine Love. And so on.

God is ever Mystery – incomprehensible. We may know
something of God, within the confines of human understanding. We cannot comprehend God. Our theological speculation
may deceive us into imagining that, somehow, we do. We issue
warnings on the hazards of God-language – on the need to
recognise that it is always analogical. It seems that we, regularly,
ignore the warnings. There has been so much talk about God
marked by an unwarranted confidence that we know what we
are talking about. We end up with a theologically neat God who
does not recognise himself in our portrait of him.

What we choose to call God is, in truth, incomprehensible
Mystery. We need all the help we can get to glimpse something
of this Mystery. The glimpse has been granted: 'Long ago God
spoke to our ancestors in many and various ways by the
prophets, but in these last days he has spoken to us by a Son'
(Hebrews 1:1-2).

Word of God

The Bible is word of God: this is acknowledged by all who take the Bible seriously. Yet, in practice, the designation – word of God – is misleading and has been, and is, the source of basic misunderstanding and has spawned a host of problems. For, if the Bible is 'word of God' – what does that mean? Only humans communicate in words. This being so, when one designates a divine communication 'word of God' one is asserting that God truly does communicate with humankind. But not only so: one asserts that the form of communication is that most common form of converse among humans, the form of language. Revelation by word of God means divine revelation which has been given human expression by humans.

God has revealed himself; he has taken the initiative, freely, lovingly. His revelation is invitation; he has revealed himself not for his own sake but always 'for us and for our salvation'. It is important to keep this in mind. We must realise that what we have come to learn of God is meant to have a bearing on our lives. In this sense, God's revelation of himself is wholly practical. Always, too, the God who has 'spoken' to us has been perceived by a human mind and communicates with us in human language. Human words are time and culturally conditioned; the same has to be of the human words of scripture. To seek to bypass the human mediator of the Word is to ignore God's way of coming to us. It is to miss the human conditioning of God's word.

The ultimate 'word' of God is neither word nor text but a person – the incarnate Son. Jesus is, indeed, 'image of the invisible God'. Even in this image God remains Holy Mystery because we humans see God in the limitation of the humanness of the Son.

Which God?

One would surely expect that the God we worship be, very firmly, God of the Bible. We may not fully appreciate the extent to which our traditional Christian image of God has been coloured by a concept of God that evolved within Greek philosophy. This Greek God is the unmoved mover, quite separated from the world. This God is so wholly transcendent, so wholly remote, that he cannot be immanent in creation. And, because in Greek thought, *to be*, in the deepest sense, meant to be altogether stable; God had to be immutable, beyond change. God is impassible, entirely free of emotion. This Greek understanding of God – and of Christ – has found expression in conciliar texts and dogmas, notably in Trinitarian and christological concern. What we, today, need to face is that the philosophical thought-world and Greek terminology of the fourth and fifth century councils of Nicaea and Chalcedon are foreign to us – in a way that the imaginative language of the Bible is not. An approach that was congenial to Christians of those centuries is not so for us. We need a theological language we can understand. As it is, our God-language still carries much of this Greek thinking. The God of our theology is, very much, a Greek God. This impassible God is not the God of the Bible.

It is time for us to claim our heritage, to acknowledge ourselves as children of the God of Abraham and Sarah – Father of our Lord Jesus Christ. The Hebrew God is a vibrant God, geared to our humanness: a *Deus humanissimus*. The Hebrew God is wholly immersed in his world; he rejoices and suffers. That implacably logical Greek God, that God of order, would be embarrassed by the sheer exuberance of a riotously evolutionary world. The Hebrew God smiles indulgently on the wondrous richness, on the overwhelming beauty: 'It is very good.' And grieves over the suffering, and the sin, that mars the goodness. Let us see something of this God.

God of Israel

Study of the Old Testament readily discovers images of God that reflect the ambient culture. In earlier religions it was regularly assumed that the gods are easily offended by human misconduct. Angered gods punish and demand propitiation. The Hebrew God punishes but is never explicitly presented as an angry God who needs to be propitiated. Sacrifice for sin was understood not as propitiation but as expiation of sin – removal of sin. That God does punish is, indeed, the view of the prophets. The imminent Babylonian invasion was, by Jeremiah and Ezekiel, firmly presented as retribution. Postexilic prayers of repentance candidly acknowledge guilt and the appropriateness of divine punitive action.

In an overall view of the Old Testament, however, that image of an angry God must not only be challenged but totally set aside. Our God is never God of wrath. When one reads the Old Testament as a whole, one meets a prodigally loving God. This is a God not remote, aloof, but a God ever with his creation. The favoured designation of Isaiah puts it in a nutshell: the Holy One of Israel. It is a brilliant recognition of the reality of God. God is transcendent, the Holy One; God is immanent, of Israel. God is never God for God's own self. God is ever God for us.

The Evolutionary God

God is Creator. Today we recognise that the God of creation is God of *ongoing* creation. Where we spoke of God as having a *plan* for the universe, we now think of God as having a *vision*. God is God of the future. Today we perceive that the universe, rather than being a settled phenomenon, is an open-ended adventure:

> This unfinished openness of natural phenomena places the world squarely within the parameters of biblical faith. For this faith forever encounters a God of promise who approaches from the future with a call to 'come ahead'. From the call of Abraham to travel to a new land, topped off by the surprising gift to him and Sarah in their old age and sterility; to the summons to the enslaved Hebrew people to cross out of Egypt into freedom; to the commission to the women disciples at the empty tomb of Jesus to go and tell the news of his resurrection: divine presence in human history is rife with surprise.[3]

God is God of freedom. God respects the freedom of creation through the gift of possibility. This sets up a relationship, based on freedom, between God and creation. God works from no detailed blueprint. He lets possibility be. Multiple finite freedoms are set free to explore their own possibilities and make their own way. God is God of love – and love does not manage the other. The world is not determined, cast in a fixed, inflexible mould. Nor is it undetermined: without plan or pattern of any sort. Rather, it is determinable: it can bend to circumstances. Only such a world provides freedom for creaturely freedom.

This in no manner implies that God is an absentee Creator – one who created and then withdrew into Olympian aloofness. God is Creator in love with his creation. He is not 'above' creation nor 'in' creation – God is *with* his creation. This is no dominating presence but one which wholly respects and preserves creaturely freedom. It is a presence of companionship, a gracious, forgiving and saving presence. This presence of God with creation is in no sense denial of the transcendence of God or of his existence independently of creation. It does imply that God is never distant or aloof. God is present with creation in all its suffering as well as in its joy.[4]

God is Creator of life that began with single-cell creatures. Humble indeed, but life intent on its own development, life intrinsically involved in its own emerging forms. Humans emerged within the evolving story. We are distinctive, yes, but firmly part of this evolving world. Growth is the purpose of life; God is God of the future. God is promise and possibility. Movement from one stage of life to another is messy and painful. Struggle is sign of new life. Failure is a necessary part of life:

> Evolution shows us that the God of becoming is a beckoning God who goes before us to invite us on, to sustain us on the way rather than a judging God who measures us by a past we did not shape ... Evolution gives us a God big enough to believe in.[5]

Relationship

Our God is Creator. We are his creatures. There, already, is relationship. From its opening, the Bible portrays God as a relational God. Our God has chosen not to remain aloof from creation. He has chosen to involve creatures in achieving his purpose for the world. In Genesis 1 we learn that God, in whole freedom, set out to bring a universe into being, a creation with its own character and potential for development. A refrain, 'God saw that it was good,' runs through the litany of creation, leading to the climactic declaration: 'God saw everything that he had made, and indeed, it was very good' (1:31). The Creator alone can say this of creation because the Creator alone sees the whole of it. The declaration does characterise the nature of God's creative work.

If we cannot really comprehend God, we can, however, have experience of God, through faith and in prayer. We can experience the love of God. Because, for us, God is personal, we speak of God in terms of the only personality we know: human personality. Like anthropomorphism, the attribution of human features to God, anthropopathism, the attribution of human feelings to God, is common in biblical language. Anthropopathism points to the *pathos* of God. The Greek term refers to what one has experienced; it surely includes experience of suffering. If we are to be true to the whole biblical picture we need to pay far more attention than we have done to language which points to the suffering of God.

Neglect of it has contributed, in its measure, to the prevailing image of God as a dominating Being. Neglect of it has caused many to turn away in disgust from a God who seems to display disdainful unconcern for human suffering. The neglect is understandable: there is no place for suffering in that detached Greek God of omnipotence and impassibility. That Greek God could never display his power and wisdom in the foolishness and weakness of the cross (see 1 Cor 1:22-25).

The language of suffering – analogical, of course – is an essential ingredient of a balanced portrait of God. It adds, immeasurably, to his attractiveness and counters, effectively, many false 'Gods' of our religious heritage. There is, surely, something compelling about a God who grieves for humankind gone astray. A God who suffers because of his people's rejection of him, who suffers with his suffering people is, indeed, a challenging God. He is, surely, the foolish God discerned by Paul. He is the God who has shown that he is a God not aloof from pain and sorrow and death. He is the God of humankind. He is the kind of God we need. He is our God. We hope to display something of this God who is the *Abba* of Jesus of Nazareth – and our *Abba* too.

CHAPTER TWO

The Holy One of Israel

For I am the Lord your God, the Holy One of Israel,
your Saviour.
(Isaiah 43:3)

Gracious Creator
In Genesis 1 we learn that God, in whole freedom, set out to
bring a universe into being, a creation with its own character
and potential for development. God created in freedom but is
always with his creation. There is, inevitably, a divine purpose
in creation. How is that purpose achieved? It is achieved in
moments where freedom and love become actual. In such moments
concurrence with God takes place. Ruth Page makes an observation that is strikingly perceptive and theologically challenging:

> God is eternal and wherever there has been concurrence
> with God, I believe that God's involvement in that moment
> makes it eternal as well ... on the other hand, divine judge-
> ment is that, although relationship is always maintained
> with every creature, where there is no concurrence, or where
> there is no renunciation of consuming selfishness, there is
> nothing to harvest. These moments come under judgement
> and fall into eternal oblivion.[1]

This makes sense – total sense. Good is always of God, and
abides. Evil disappears into its own nothingness. This is reminiscent of Aquinas' insistence that evil is the absence of good:
malum est privatio boni.

God's Need
God's creative deed is free. God had, absolutely, no need of the
universe, no need of humankind. But he did bring us into being.
As a result one can say, with truth, that humankind is necessary
to God – necessary in the sense that a deed of God has to be

meaningful. Creation was not a whim. God was in deadly earnest. There lies our hope, our assurance. God has made us for himself, has called us to be his children. God waits for our response. God needs us; needs us to know our need of him. A lesser God would have made a better job of it! He would have created beings who could not but acknowledge their dependence and be wholly thankful to their Creator. Our God has no time for slaves. His only weapon is love. His children will be freely his children. Only a God who is God would call into being creatures who might say No! to their Creator.

God is Creator of a universe. While we humans, with God's help, discern our place in his purpose, we have tended to be self-centred. Have we not been prone to regard ourselves as, in some sort, focus of God's well-nigh exclusive attention? And, in our tiny corner of this vast world, we have acted, and do act, as though all else on our planet were solely for our use and benefit. We need a humbler view, a more realistic view. Humility is truth.

Gracious Creator

God is a *gracious* Creator. God is not mean-minded. Today we have a perception, far beyond that of the biblical writers, of the well-nigh incredible grandeur of creation. We become more and more aware of the sheer vastness of the universe – a vastness that boggles the imagination. God has created with appropriately divine abandon. Our awe before the vast spread of the universe leads to awe of the Creator. There is an even greater wonder. It is the assurance that this Almighty Creator, with a near infinite universe within his ken, has whole concern for humans on our puny planet: 'What are human beings that you are mindful of them, mortals that you care for them?' (Psalm 8:4). God has *divine* concern for us. This is not only our comfort – it is a measure of the true divinity of our God. The psalmist grasped and expressed the gracious magnanimity of the Creator when, in a tone of awe, he exclaimed of God's creation of humankind: 'You have made them a little less than God!' (8:5).

The God of the Bible, the Father of our Lord Jesus Christ, is the foolish God (see 1 Cor 1:18-21). His gamble was in making us free. He stands, stolidly, by that gamble. God is, happily, not an Unmoved Mover. God is not even Creator. God is Parent.

And just there is the divine vulnerability. What loving parent can ever, ever reject the child? Our human grace is not that we are creatures of God, not even that we are image of God. The ultimate divine foolishness, made emphatic in Christian revelation, is that we are children of God. That is Christian truth – but it must reach to all of humanity.

Parent
Traditionally, our God is Father. Our God-language, including the God-language of scripture, is emphatically male. Our God-image is andromorphic – male-imaged. Because the Bible itself comes out of and reflects a patriarchal culture, it tends to be androcentric, male-centred. The predominant biblical images for God are taken from male experience, with God being depicted as Father, King, Warrior and so on. At the same time there is an intriguing openness to female imagery, with God being imaged as birth-giving woman and loving mother (see Deut 33:18; Is 42:14; 66:13). In point of fact, it makes as much sense to refer to God as Mother as it does to call God 'Father'. God is neither male nor female; God stands apart from such categories – God is transcendent.[2] To call God 'Father' is to acknowledge that God is the source of our being, of our life, in a measure that is, in some fashion, comparable to our parents' role: they bring us into being and care for us. In that sense, God is Parent. But we do not know what divine 'parenthood' might mean – except that it must outstrip, infinitely, in graciousness, the most lovable human parental relationship.

Indeed, at its best, human parental love can be a thing of wonder. For instance, there is the self-sacrificing loving care of a severely handicapped child. It is by bringing together father-love and mother-love that we arrive at the fullness of parental love. In view of this, surely, 'parent' is the term most appropriate to convey an inkling of divine love. God is *parent*. And just there is divine vulnerability. What loving parent can ever, ever reject the child? There is the comforting assurance of Isaiah 49:15:

> Can a woman forget her nursing child, or show contempt for the child of her womb?
> Even these may forget,
> yet I will never forget you.

Our human grace is not that we are creatures of God; not even that we are image of God. The ultimate divine foolishness, made emphatic in Christian revelation, is that we are *children* of God.

Children

God is a gracious Creator who loves his creation. God has created freely and with abandon. We may look no further than our own planet. The author of the Book of Wisdom observed: 'The goodness and beauty of created things give us a corresponding idea of the Creator' (Wis 13:5).

In creation, as we know it, humankind is God's masterpiece. God has, with divine graciousness, called us to be his children. What has been our response? Novelist Paul Gallico asks:

> Supposing God *had* made man, not in his own image, but in some reflection of his own love and spirit and turned him loose on earth to work out his own destiny. Must not his heart, must not any great creative, all-embracing heart be wrung with compassion for what his children had turned out to be?[3]

There is grief and sadness in the heart of God. There is no wrath, no anger. Only in our perversity do we imagine an angry God. After all, children, especially teenage children, tend to regard the care and concern of parents as oppressive. With regard to our Parent, we have been rebellious teenagers. With infinite patience God deals with us, not infringing on our freedom, but respecting our dignity. God is saddened at seeing us enslave ourselves to other gods. Our Parent is saddened at the harm we have done to ourselves, to others, to the whole of his earthly creation, grieved at the sheer burden of sin that weighs upon us. Our Parent is constantly calling out to us: 'Here am I, here am I' (Is 65:1). God waits for our response, waits not only with patience but with divine compassion.

Humankind

'What are human beings that you are mindful of them, mortals that you care for them? ... you have made them a little less than God' (Ps 8:4-5). The psalmist gazed on the broad sweep of the sky and across the Earth to the distant horizon. He looked at puny humans and wondered: '… you have made *them* little less than gods!' We realise that earth is but one planet in our galaxy, that it is an infinitesimally tiny speck in a vast universe. And we wonder that the Creator of the universe chooses not to be alone. There may be other creatures in other worlds with whom he has dialogue. We do not know. But we do know that God has called humankind into being, freely and of set purpose. Freely – because freedom is an essential attribute of God; freedom is of supreme value to our God. God has made us free and he meticulously respects our freedom. Often one hears the complaint: If God be God, why is our world in such a mess? Why does he not take steps to clean up the mess? The answer is, precisely, God's respect for human freedom. God might wave a magic wand. The cost is too high and he will not exact the price: the sacrifice of freedom. God might have programmed our world. But he does not choose to converse with robots. 'Is the arm of the Lord shortened?' (Is 50:2). The course of history might suggest that God has lost control of his creation. The truth is, the verdict on creation – 'God saw everything that he had made, and indeed, it was very good' (Gen 1:31) – is a verdict that God alone can pass. We glimpse but 'the outskirts of his ways' (Job 26:13). God has had the first word. God will have the last.

Promise and Covenant

Now the Lord said to Abram, 'Go from your country and your kindred and your father's house to the land that I will show you' (Gen 12:1).

Abraham was chosen and called – the 'scandal' of election. He was called to serve the divine purpose, and in this service the scandal is resolved. Abraham was called to break with his natural ties: country, clan and family. He was to get up and go 'to the land that I will show you'. The author of Hebrews has a perceptive comment: 'By faith, Abraham obeyed when he was called to set out for a place that he was to receive as an inheritance; and he set out, not knowing where he was going' (Heb 11:8). If God will have the last word, humankind must accept that it is so.

'I will make of you a great nation' (Gen 12:2). The word is *goy*

('nation') and not *am* ('people'); *goy* is a political term and requires a territorial base. Abraham came into the land of Canaan
and there at last he was told of the goal – a telling that was word
of promise. 'Then the Lord appeared to Abram, and said, "To
your offspring I will give this land" (12:7).' Promise leads to
covenant. In the primitive covenant ritual of Genesis 15 it is
made abundantly clear that the land is gift and is received as
gift. The covenant rests on God's initiative and his unconditional
promise and asks only for trust. Twice more will Abraham hear
that word of promise (17:8; 24:7), and promise it will remain for
him and his descendants for generations to come. The story of
creation and the story of Abraham were both written in the light
of Exodus-faith. The God of Israel is always the God who immersed himself in the life of his people.

God had promised his people a land. But the promise of the
land is rooted in paradox. The beginning of salvation-history
sees a landed man, Abraham, called from city and country and
launched into a situation of landlessness. The one who receives
the promise of the land (Gen 12:1) will himself, henceforth, live
as a landless wanderer. He is sustained by that promise alone.
And so it will be for his successors. The land of Goshen (Gen
47:27) could never be their abiding home. It was in the desert
that Israel would learn to know Yahweh. It has been ever so.
Only when one has dared to look at what really matters – and
'desert' is a radical symbol – can one discover the true God. It is
like the fox's secret in *The Little Prince*: 'And now here is my secret, a very simple secret: it is only with the heart that one sees
rightly; what is essential is invisible to the eye'.[4]

From the start, Abraham was a man of faith. Yahweh was
fully aware of the difficulty of what was asked: Abraham must
leave everything. Later, despite his advanced age and that of a
sterile Sarah, Abraham put his faith in Yahweh, confident that
he will, somehow, be ancestor of numberless descendants (Gen
15:5-6). Then, there is that 'sacrifice': his readiness to sacrifice
the child of promise, Isaac (22:1-19). A poignant story indeed.
The tragic dignity of Abraham and his readiness to give his own
son stirred a Christian sentiment. The deed of Abraham has
surely coloured the telling of a greater love: 'He who did not
withhold his own Son, but gave him up for all of us' (Rom 8:32);

'God so loved the world that he gave his only Son' (Jn 3:16). Abraham had put his faith in God, a seemingly capricious and callous God. For, Abraham saw, what Paul and John were to recognise, that his God, however unpredictable, is to be trusted. God can make outrageous demands because he will ever be faithful. As regards Abraham, the verdict of Paul stands: 'Abraham is a man of faith' (Gal 3:6-9; Rom 4:1-3).

Moses
God had called Abraham from a welter of nations and had given him the assurance that in him 'all the families of the earth shall be blessed' (Gen 12:3). That solemn promise seemed to have foundered in Egyptian bondage (Exodus 1). God will not be gainsaid. As he had called Abraham, now he sends Moses (Ex 3-4). He guided his way and through him delivered his people. That people, on the safe shore of the Red Sea, sang in joyful jubilation to the Lord (Ex 15:1-18). The song resounds with the conviction of a people that had understood that their God was ever the God of the Exodus. The poet, who knew of the unfaithfulness and rebellion of the desert wanderings, had come to accept that it would be the pattern of Israel's future conduct. More significantly, he had discerned, sharply focused against a people's infidelity, the faithfulness of his God:

> In your steadfast love you led the people you had redeemed; you guided them by your strength to your holy abode (15:13).

The historical exodus was a petty affair. What really took place is lost forever within the core of a great religious saga. In Exodus 1-15 we read the birth-story of Israel as a people. The whole of Exodus tells of Israel's understanding of itself and of its faith. That faith of Israel had discerned in Yahweh's concern for oppressed slaves the true character of a God of salvation. The Exodus-saga reflects a long and chequered dialogue between God and people. Today, enlightened by insights of liberation theology, we can observe that the exodus event – and this remains true even in the saga – was, first and last, a sociological and political event. Slaves were set free from slavery, delivered from 'a house of bondage' and, eventually, led to a homeland.

Later, the poet Second Isaiah, in his drumming-up of some
enthusiasm for a return from Babylonian exile, casts the return
to freedom as a new Exodus (Is 40:3-11). The archetypal redemption event was, essentially, a liberation. It is a salutary reminder
that our God is not in the business of saving 'souls'; he wants to
set people free. Salvation has to do with humanness, every
aspect of true humanness.

Moses had led the first pilgrimage of the people of God: a journey from slavery to freedom. In biblical tradition Egypt would
remain a symbol of oppression and bondage. The land of Palestine
would function as a promise fulfilled. Even when the land was
lost, it would re-emerge as a promise of restoration. The pilgrimage was a rough passage and not only because of desert hardship.
Throughout Exodus, more markedly in Numbers, there is a struggle between God and people with Moses at the heart of the mael-
strom. He did not emerge unscathed (Num 20:12). Yet it was he
who put his finger – in a challenge to his God – on the abiding
characteristic of the God of the Bible, the goal of pilgrimage:

> Forgive the iniquity of this people according to the greatness
> of your steadfast love, just as you have pardoned this people,
> from Egypt even until now (Num 14:19).

> If my God is not a God of steadfast love – he is not God.

Covenant

> I will establish my covenant between me and you, and
> your offspring after you throughout their generations, for
> an everlasting covenant, to be God to you and to your off-
> spring after you (Gen 17:7).

In the Old Testament there are two different understandings of
covenant. The covenant with Abraham is a *promissory* covenant.
Yahweh bestows the covenant as gift. This is strikingly presented
in Genesis 15 where Abraham is wholly passive (v 12) as Yahweh
performs the covenant rite. The later covenant with David is just
such a promissory covenant: 'The Lord declares to you that the
Lord will make you a house' (2 Sam 7:11). The Sinai covenant, on
the other hand, is *conditional*: 'I am your God and you are my people *if* …'. This is developed in the theology of Deuteronomy:

See, I set before you today life and prosperity, death and adversity. If you obey the commandments of the Lord your
God that I am commanding you today ... then you shall live
and become numerous, and the Lord your God will bless
you ... But if your heart turns away and you do not hear ... I
declare to you today that you shall perish (Deut 30:15-18).

Fragile Theology
The eighth century prophet Isaiah was rooted in the traditions
of Jerusalem and David and firmly believed in the promise
made to David. For, in Judah, the Davidic covenant (2 Sam 7)
had replaced that of Sinai, and Zion with its temple was the new
holy mountain. Hope for the future rested in the Davidic line:
'Your house and your kingdom shall be made sure for ever before me; your throne shall be established for ever' (2 Sam 7:16).
The king of Judah was 'son of God' (7:14). No condition attached
to the promise to David. Though individual kings might fail, the
dynasty would be eternal. Yahweh would dwell forever among
his people, would reign on Mount Zion. He would be their
shield against their foes; no enemy could destroy the holy city
and the blessed dynasty. This conviction was the theological
basis of Isaiah's hope in the face of seemingly inevitable disaster. Because of it he could assure Hezekiah that Sennacherib and
his Assyrians would never take the city of David (Is 37:3-35).

A century after Isaiah, when Judah was threatened by
Babylon, the prophet Jeremiah was to face an impossible task in
striving to convince his contemporaries that Nebuchadnezzar,
unlike Sennacherib, would have his way and that Zion and its
temple would perish. He was not believed. What Yahweh had
done in the days of Hezekiah he would surely continue to do.
The son of David was son of Yahweh; Zion was city of Yahweh;
the temple was his dwelling-place. A young Jeremiah could
have adhered to that theology, the comforting theology of a
promissory covenant. Always there was another, and an older,
view of God's covenant with his people. Though the Sinai
covenant had, at least in Judah, slipped into the background, it
had not passed from sight. Here was no unconditional promise.
Israel had been granted a covenant and had accepted the stipul-

ations of the Lord. An older Jeremiah, faced with the patent failure of the Davidic monarchy, looked back to the Sinai covenant.
What he was sure of, in the teeth of disaster, was that Yahweh
could and would pick up the pieces and put them together
again. Yahweh could do what 'all the king's horses and all the
king's men' could not do.

For Isaiah the traditional theology could still work. For
Jeremiah, not in a very different situation, it no longer made
sense. He had to look for another theology, one that really met
his situation. Isaiah had looked for an Immanuel, the ideal
Davidic king. He would never have recognised that future king
in a helpless victim on a cross. One feels that Jeremiah might
have met him there. Isaiah, when put in perspective, alerts one
to the fragility of any tidy theological system. God will not be
confined. He must be allowed to surprise us. While our faith
should grow in firmness, our theology should ever be open,
open to the breath of the Spirit, alert to the 'signs of the time'.

In short, it must be said that Jeremiah did flatly contradict
the popular belief in Yahweh's eternal and unconditional choice
of Mount Zion. This finds emphatic expression in the so-called
'Temple sermon' (Jer 7:1-15). There was, then, a collision in theology, a clash of two ways of viewing the nation's election and relation to God. One stressed God's unfailing promises which
nothing could cancel; the other stressed his righteous commandments which no one might disregard with impunity. On
the one hand, there was God's promise to Abraham and to
David: this nation and this dynasty will always endure. On the
other hand, there was the covenant in the desert with its stipula-
tions which firmly obliged the nation: the nation can be, and
will be, destroyed because it has broken covenant with Yahweh.

It is clear that Jeremiah was right and his opponents were
wrong. Does this mean that the theology of the Mosaic covenant
was right and theology of covenant promises was wrong? John
Bright puts it aptly:

> The Mosaic covenant reminded Israel of God's grace to her
> which had saved her and made her his people, and of her
> obligation to live in obedience to his commandments if she
> wished to continue in his favour and receive his blessing.

The promises to Abraham and to David assured her that, in the final analysis, her future rested ultimately not in what she was – or had, or had not, done – but in the sure immutable purposes of God which nothing could cancel. Without the one, Israel could not have been God's people; without the other, she might well have lived – to despair.[5]

It is notable that, in the New Age, Paul firmly set the promissory covenant with Abraham above the Sinai covenant (Gal 4:21-31; Rom 4). And his firm conviction that 'all Israel will be saved' was based on the premise that 'the gifts and the call of God are irrevocable' (Rom 11:26, 29).

The New Covenant
The Sinai covenant was conditional on the people's ability to obey the law – and the people had failed to obey. Jeremiah, beyond the disaster, proclaimed a whole new basis for covenant:

> The days are surely coming, says the Lord, when I will make a new covenant with the house of Israel and the house of Judah. It will not be like the covenant that I made with their ancestors when I took them by the hand to bring them out of the land of Egypt – a covenant that they broke … But this is the covenant that I will make with the house of Israel after those days, says the Lord: I will put my law within them, and I will write it on their hearts; and I will be their God, and they shall be my people (Jer 31:31-33).

What is new is that there is a change in the relationship between God and people. God will give them a new heart; they will respond in good faith and trusting obedience. Jeremiah's own experience is reflected here. He had preached to a hopelessly obdurate people; he is convinced that God must take a hand and change the human heart (see 32:37-41). He glimpsed the era of the Spirit as Paul will characterise it: the 'law of the Spirit of life' (Rom 8:2). And, on that night before the Lord went to his death, he brought the most solemn promise of the prophet to fulfilment: 'This cup is the new covenant in my blood' (Lk 22:20).

The God of the Old Testament is the Holy One of Israel, a God transcendent and immanent. One might term the Old

Testament the book of Two Constancies. There is the constancy of human unfaithfulness, documented with refreshing candour. And there is the accompanying, and prevailing, constancy of divine faithfulness. God will be faithful – no matter what. Indeed, one senses a gut-feeling: Israel's innate persuasion that God, having freely chosen Israel, is stuck with Israel! It is surely the conviction of that proud Israelite, Paul: 'God has not rejected his people whom he foreknew' – because 'the gifts and the calling of God are irrevocable' (Rom 11:2, 29).

CHAPTER THREE

Justice

Since there will never cease to be some in need on the earth,
I therefore command you, 'Open your hand to the poor and
needy neighbour in your land.' (Deuteronomy 15:11)

If we are to speak of God at all, we must speak in human terms.
Too readily we seem to lose sight of the fact that God-language
is always analogical and we begin to take anthropomorphism
literally. We can, and do, make statements about God that make
human sense. But, no expression for God can be taken literally.
This because we cannot know God in God's own self. I can say,
with truth, that God is a loving God. I speak out of my experience of human love. Though I have not an inkling of the reality
of divine love, my assertion is not meaningless. Again, my
experience of justice is human justice. And here we begin to go
hopelessly wrong. Our just God is reduced to our level.
Accordingly, we have come up with a God who condemns sinners to hell – and rightly so! The error is when what reasonably
operates as justice on the human level is taken to be operative in
the world of God. Consider this statement: 'God is a just God,
who deals with us fairly.' By human standards, impeccable. But
… does any of us wish to be treated *fairly* by God? Do we want
our God to deal with us as we truly deserve? Surely, we hope to
be treated with loving mercy. And that is how our just God does
treat us – because divine justice *is* mercy. We need to look to the
biblical understanding of justice.

Justice

In Exodus 3:13-15, the anonymous God of Abraham, Isaac and
Jacob revealed himself to Moses as Yahweh. It marks a new turn
in God's concern for humankind. Walter Brueggemann claims
that the main force of this 'Mosaic revolution' was 'to establish
justice as the core focus of Yahweh's life in the world and
Israel's life with Yahweh.'[1] The two main features of the Mosaic

revolution are the event of the Exodus and the Sinai proclamation of Yahweh's commandments. The central fact of Exodus was the freeing of Hebrew slaves from Egyptian bondage. The contest with Pharaoh shows a God committed to the establishment of a system of justice in a regime organised against justice. It is noteworthy that Yahweh acted in response to the suffering of slaves:

> The Israelites groaned under their slavery and cried out ... God heard their groaning ... God looked upon the Israelites and God took notice of them (Ex 2:22-23). I have observed the misery of my people who are in Egypt ... I know their sufferings, and I have come down to deliver them (3:7-8).

The second feature is the Sinai proclamation of Yahweh's commandments (Ex 20:1-21; see 20:12–23:13). As they worked themselves out in the life and religious traditions of Israel, the Exodus event and the Sinai institution do indeed bear witness to Yahweh's preferential option for the poor, the weak and the marginalised. Yahweh's passion for justice is meant to be implemented concretely in human practice. It is essential to be quite clear that what is at issue is *distributive* justice. This means the redistribution of social goods and the sharing of power. It is the awareness that the wellbeing of a community requires that possessions be, to an extent, given up by the wealthy for the sake of those who do not have enough, and power tempered by the powerful in favour of the powerless. Israel understood that such conduct was a demand of Yahweh.

We are more familiar with a different concept of justice: *retributive* justice. It means giving to persons what is their just desert on the basis of performance. So, for instance, the notion of a just wage and of punishment of misconduct – in general, a system of reward and punishment. While retributive justice was indeed recognised in Israel, emphasis is, undoubtedly, on distributive justice. This is not to say that the consequent obligation was always or predominantly carried through in practice. In Israel, as in every society, there was tension between 'haves' and 'have-nots'. There were staunch advocates of a status quo that favoured the privileged. Yet 'there can be little doubt that the adherents of distributive justice occupy the central space in the ideological testimony of Israel, so that in canonical Yahwism, distributive justice is indeed a primary urging'.[2] Remarkable across the different Old Testament traditions is an insistence on the obligation to care for those too weak to protect themselves. There is the basic principle expressed in Deuteronomy 15:11:

> Since there will never cease to be some in need on the earth, I therefore command you, 'Open your hand to the poor and needy neighbour in your land.'

That there will always be poor is realistic acknowledgment of our sinful human situation. It is no fatalistic acceptance. It is a challenge. The poor and the needy are regularly named as 'the strangers, the orphans and the widows' (see Deut 16:11, 14; 14:19-21; 26:12-15; Is 1:17; Jer 7:6; 22:3; Zech 7:10). Concern for them is rooted in the character of Yahweh who is 'Father of orphans and protector of widows' (Ps 68:5).

Israel's preoccupation with justice is notably evident in the prophets. It resounds in the celebrated demand of Micah:

> He has told you, O mortal, what is good;
> and what does the Lord require of you
> But to do justice and to love kindness,
> and to walk humbly with your God (6:8).

This verse brings together the main themes of Amos (justice), Hosea (loving kindness) and Isaiah (humble trust in God). Justice here is, primarily, vindication of the poor and the needy, of the marginalised. This is the burden of the call:

> Seek good and not evil that you may live …
> Hate evil and love good, and establish justice in the gate (Amos 5:14-15).

The 'gate', where the elders of a town heard complaints and settled cases, is, in effect, the law-court. And the concern is that the rights of the poor be upheld.

The eighth-century prophet Amos was the great champion of justice. He firmly proclaimed and vindicated the moral order established by God and enshrined in the covenant. He castigated the abuses that prevailed in an era of hectic prosperity – the reign of Jeroboam II in Israel. To his eyes the symptoms of social decay were glaring. Wealth, concentrated in the hands of a few, and these the leaders of the people, had corrupted its possessors. Oppression of the poor was rife. The richly-endowed national religion, with its elaborate ritual, induced a comfortable, self-righteous atmosphere. The prophet set out to shatter this dangerous complacency. It is not surprising that Amos is a favourite of the theologians of liberation. The prophet, in the name of his God, spoke out, not only against the situation of his day, but against injustice in any age. God is always on the side of the oppressed. And God will not be mocked. The rulers of Israel felt assured that they had reached the Promised land. The prophet would insist that they occupied a fool's paradise.

What justice is, is stated with great force in the latter part of Isaiah – Is 56-66 (sixth century). Even among the returned exiles, division and dissension soon emerged. Too quickly, religion became an escape-hatch. But, God is not fooled:

> Day after day they seek me and delight to know my ways,
> as if they were a nation that practised righteousness and did
> not forsake the ordinance of their God (58:2).

There was, evidently, an emphasis on religious observance. It seems that ritual fasting was in vogue. God is not impressed:

> Is not this the fast that I choose:
> to loose the bonds of injustice,
> to undo the thongs of the yoke,
> to let the oppressed go free,
> and to break every yoke?
> Is it not to share your bread with the hungry,
> and bring the homeless poor into your house ...
> Then your light shall break forth like the dawn,
> and your healing shall spring up quickly (58:6-8).

What God chooses is the 'fast' of justice – he will have nothing less.

In practice, this biblical preoccupation with distributive justice has been downplayed or ignored. And the justice of God has been heard as retributive justice. Consequently, God has been cast as Judge who, along the line of retributive justice, hands out reward and punishment. We speak glibly of God as a just Judge.

Well it is for us that God is *unjust*. We have tended to categorise sin as crime. So, we 'break' the commandments. We commonly referred to the sacrament of reconciliation as the 'tribunal of penance'. In this setting, a repentant sinner is a criminal appearing before a judge. Very well – what happens? If God be Judge, he is the Judge who acquits the guilty – those who enter a plea of 'guilty' – the repentant sinner. It is not a matter of handing down a lenient sentence or a suspended sentence. No; the judge simply accepts the plea of guilty (acknowledgment of sin) – and dismisses the case (forgiveness). A human judge who would act so, could not expect to hold his job for long. But God is doing it all the time (see Mt 18:24-27). We should rejoice in the *injustice* of our God. Indeed, we might question the propriety of imaging God as judge at all. *We* seem to have a problem in our striving to reconcile God's mercy with God's justice. Let us not lose any sleep over it: *God* has no such problem.

Wrath

The prophets of Israel proposed no theory of God, did not seek to expound the nature of God. They offered instead God's understanding of humankind and his concern for humanity. Very particularly, they had an insight into the *pathos* of God – the Greek term refers to experience, to being intrinsically affected by events or persons. Pathos is not an attribute of God. It is an expression of God's loving care for his creation; it marks a God involved in history. The fundamental concern of the Bible is not creation but God's care for creation. The basic feature of pathos is divine attentiveness and concern. Above all, it is the divine attentiveness to humanity. Indeed, it is through his pathos, his relation to Israel and to humanity, that we can know God at all. We can think of God only insofar as God thinks of us. God thinks of us always with concern. The dominant pathos of God is love or mercy. But, there is also the pathos of wrath.

It is undeniable that scripture does speak of the 'wrath' of God. God's 'anger' is an aspect of divine pathos; it is as response to human sin. The biblical term 'anger' denotes what we call righteous indignation. It is impatience with evil. Psalm 7:11 puts it like this: 'God is a righteous judge, and a God who has indignation every day.' In the Bible, a judge is not merely a person

competent to consider a case and pronounce sentence, but one
who is pained and distressed by injustice:

> It is because God cares for humanity that his anger may be
> kindled against humans. Anger and mercy are not opposites
> but correlatives. Thus Habakkuk prays: 'In wrath remember
> mercy' (3:2). It is inconceivable that God's love should ever
> cease.[3]

The pathos of anger is never regarded as an attribute of God,
but as a response of God. In its origin and in its duration it is
clearly distinguished from mercy. This is beautifully expressed
in Isaiah 54:7-8:

> For a brief moment I abandoned you,
> but with great compassion I will gather you.
> In overflowing wrath for a moment I hid my face from you,
> but with everlasting love I will have compassion on you,
> says the Lord your Redeemer.

'Brief moment' – 'great compassion'; wrath 'for a moment' –
'everlasting love': there is a radical imbalance. Compassion
flows from the love of a Redeemer. 'Wrath' is the grieving of a
spurned Parent.

There is a biblical belief in divine grace, divine compassion.
There is no belief in abiding and consuming divine anger. What
is often proclaimed of love, for instance the refrain of Psalm
136 – 'for his steadfast love endures forever' – is never said
about anger. The normal and original pathos is love, mercy. It is
only in the certainty that God's mercy is greater than his justice
that the prophet could pray:

> Although our iniquities testify against us,
> Act, O Lord, for your name's sake (Jer 14:7).[4]

We shall see that, far from being a God of 'wrath', our God is
a God who suffers.

Suffering God

Our traditional God is an aloof figure – often a forbidding figure. Strangely, while he is firmly presented as one gravely offended by human sin, he has been made to appear unaffected by

human suffering. There is an appalling burden of suffering. It is a devastating fact that stands as an indictment. How can suffering on such a scale – so much innocent suffering to boot – be compatible with faith in a benevolent Creator? The question is a tormenting one. If one's God is stolidly impassible there can be no answer short of a blind and desperate act of faith. Yet, there is an answer (insofar as there can be an answer that makes some human sense). Biblical metaphor demands that we acknowledge a God who grieves and laments and suffers.

If we are to be true to the *whole* biblical picture, we shall need to pay far more attention than we had to metaphors of *pathos*. Neglect of them has contributed, in its measure, to the prevailing image of God as a dominating Being. Neglect of them has caused many to turn away, in disgust, from a God who seems to display disdainful unconcern for human suffering. Attention to them would surely have fostered a more caring church and might have tempered ecclesiastical arrogance. Perhaps. Most importantly, these metaphors of pathos are essential ingredients of a balanced portrait of God. They add, immeasurably, to his attractiveness and counter, effectively, the many false gods of our religious heritage.

God had chosen Israel as his own and had made a covenant with his people. Now, he suffers when he is spurned and rejected by his people. He suffers because he is, and will be, faithful. He recalls his promise to Noah and rephrases it, in stronger terms, in favour of Israel:

> As I swore that the waters of Noah
> should no more go over the earth,
> so I have sworn that I will not be angry with you …
> My steadfast love shall not depart from you … (Is 54:9-10).

God will poignantly conjure up what might have been. The Book of Isaiah, for instance, opens on a note of bewilderment:

> Children have I raised and brought up,
> but they have rebelled against me.
> The ox knows its owner,
> and the donkey its master's crib;
> but Israel does not know,
> my people does not understand (1:2-3).

God spoke as Parent, cut to the heart by the ingratitude of children. And God suffers the pang of unrequited love:

> I thought you would call me, My Father,
> and would not turn from following me.
> Surely, as a faithless wife leaves her husband,
> so have you been faithless to me, O house of Israel (Jer 3:20).

Here the easy juxtaposition of parent-child and husband-wife metaphors alerts us to the common theme of love and assures us that a loving God experiences the pain as well as the rapture of love. Notable throughout the prophets is reference to the spurning of parental love. God suffers, and sorrows over, the pain inflicted by ungracious and ungrateful children. God remains the loving Parent who will never abandon those children.

> But Zion said, 'The Lord has forsaken me, my Lord has forgotten me.'
> Can a woman forget her nursing child,
> or show no compassion for the child of her womb?
> Even these may forget, but I will not forget you (Is 49:14-15).

Here is mother pathos at the heart of God: she loves her child and will not, because she cannot, let go. God's suffering is not for herself; it is for the erring and suffering child – a rebellious people.

> God is not simply father; God is a certain kind of father. God is a loving father, always (Hos 11:1). And God is not simply mother; God is a certain kind of mother. God is a mother who will not forget her child, ever (Is 49:15).[5]

God is never one who stands calmly aloof, impervious to being spurned and rejected by his people. He is one who grieves over a broken relationship – grieves for the tragic ungrateful partner. God treats the human party in the relationship with total seriousness and scrupulously respects human freedom. His patience is inexhaustible; he cannot be worn down. He may withdraw, but he will not finally give up. The breach will be healed.

God has given voice to his pain at his people's rejection of him, his sorrow that the people, by and large, had gone astray. Israel was his people: I am your God, you are my people. He had established a covenant with his people – 'my covenant, which you broke'. They had spurned him, had gone their own way. Their stubbornness could not wear him down. Paul had understood when, against all logic, he maintained: 'all Israel will be saved.' Why? 'Because the gifts and the call of God are irrevocable' (Rom 11:36, 29). There is the comfort for humans. All are called to be children of God. He is faithful, though all prove unfaithful. He is ever Parent, though we be fickle children.

God is God of compassion – he suffers with his suffering children. Human pain, human woe, are not of his devising. Pain is of the web and woof of human life – not a punishment imposed on humankind. 'Behold, it is very good.' God alone can see the whole of creation – 'good', that is, purposeful. Pain and death are part of that world – not only of the human world. Why? There is mystery. To view pain and death as punishment inflicted by a 'just' God is to demean God. That has been the way of religious tradition. We honour God by accepting our human lot as challenge, challenge to look above and raise our eyes beyond pain and mortality. We are helped, immeasurably, if we look to a God of compassion who is with us in our woe and in our death. He is the God who waits to wipe away all tears. Like little children we come, tear-stained, to our God that she may comfort. A little child may not know why she or he may hurt – but knows that there is solace, and the pain is forgotten. But the pain is real.

Strangest of all, most comforting of all, God bears the burden of human sin. That is God's decision after the Flood (Gen 8:21). He is wearied by human sin; he bears with it. Birth, new life, comes out of pain. God is pregnant with life, Mother of new creation. There is one answer only to the evil that is sin – and to all evil. Violence can never be the answer. Nothing but love, the infinitely patient divine love, can absorb evil and put it out of commission. God does not suffer in silence. He protests against any manipulation of him. But he suffers – in the manner in which *God* may suffer. He feels and shares the pain inflicted in his name on the weak and vulnerable. So many have been broken, so many have been shattered, in the name of God. Throughout history, to our day, God has been dishonoured. He has been wearied beyond measure. Because too often and with frightening consistency, religious observance has been denial of or suppression of human values. Any depreciation of human values is denial of the God of humankind.

The language of suffering – analogical, of course – is an essential ingredient of a balanced portrait of God. It adds, immeasurably, to his attractiveness and counters, effectively many false 'Gods' of our religious heritage. There is, surely, something compelling about a God who grieves for humankind gone astray. A God who suffers because of his people's rejection of him, who suffers with his suffering people, who suffers on behalf of the people, is, indeed, a challenging God. He is, surely the foolish God discerned by Paul. He is the God who has shown that he is a God not aloof from pain and sorrow and death. He is the kind of God we need. He is *our* God.

CHAPTER FOUR

Mercy

O Lord! Is not this what I said while I was still in my own country? That is why I fled to Tarshish at the beginning; for I know that you are a gracious God and merciful, slow to anger, and abiding in steadfast love. (Jonah 4:2)

Our tendency is to limit the reach of God's love. Sadly, a loving Parent suffers misunderstanding and ingratitude. The misunderstanding reaches to scandal at the Parent's mercy to sinners. There seems to be a rooted human reluctance to acknowledge and wholeheartedly welcome a gracious God – in particular when that graciousness is directed to others.

The story of Jonah – a brilliant short story – mounts a protest. It tells of a reluctant prophet. Sent with a message of warning to Nineveh, capital of the Assyrian empire (very definitely to the east of Palestine), Jonah headed west – 'away from the presence of the Lord'. He had a nagging suspicion that, in sending him with stern warning to the Ninevites, his God had a hidden agenda. He feared that mercy and forgiveness might lurk within the word of threat. His worst fears were realised. God relented and spared the repentant Ninevites (3:10). 'But this was very displeasing to Jonah' (4:1).

The tragedy of his stance is caught up in one astonishing statement:

He prayed to the Lord and said, 'O Lord! Is not this what I said while I was still in my own country? That is why I fled to Tarshish at the beginning: for I knew that you are a gracious God and merciful, slow to anger, and abounding in steadfast love, and ready to relent from punishing. And now, O Lord, please take my life from me, for it is better for me to die than to live' (4:2-3).

Jonah had fled his God. That was grave indeed. The enormity is that he had fled this *God* – a God gracious, merciful, of stead-

fast love! There is the rub: infinite love, a love that knew no
limit, no frontier. It was a love that embraced even the hated
Ninevites. This was too much. In Johannine terms, 'This is a
hard saying, who can accept it?' (Jn 6:60). It is all too reminiscent
of the reaction to the word and the praxis of Jesus: 'This fellow
welcomes sinners and eats with them' (Lk 15:2). It is never easy
for the 'righteous' to come to terms with an 'unjust' God. Jonah,
then, underlines the predictable human reaction to divine generosity. If God is gracious to me – fine. He dare not be gracious
to those whom we have judged to be undeserving of his mercy.[1]

God and Sin

The story of the Flood (Genesis 6-9) is of major theological significance. It dramatises the destructive nature of sin and the reaction of God to sin. The strange episode of 'the sons of God and
the daughters of humans' (6:1-4) is meant to mark a stage, far beyond that of the man and woman of Genesis 3, in the futile
human striving 'to be like God' – to be independent of God.
What is in question here is wholesale corruption – to such a de-
gree as to threaten human existence. God has to do something
about the situation. 'And the Lord was sorry that he had made
humankind on the earth, and it grieved him to his heart' (6:6).
Though his reaction is grief and sorrow, God unleashes the
flood waters. God suffers the pain of a grieving parent, yet his
reaction is thorough and uncompromising.

The seeming contradiction is resolved in the purpose of the
story. This purpose begins to emerge at the turning point: 'God
remembered Noah' (8:1). From a path of destruction there is a
turn to salvation. The story ends in hope and promise:

> I establish my covenant with you, that never again shall all
> flesh be cut off by the waters of the flood, and never again
> shall there be a flood to destroy the earth (9:11).

Throughout the Flood story we are in the presence of myth:
an expression of universal truth in 'historical' terms. It is a para-
digm of an ongoing biblical concern. God represents infinite
love and mercy and forgiveness. He wills the salvation of all.
God would certainly not launch a flood to destroy not only sinful humankind but all earthly life. God is Creator, source and

sustainer of life; he is not in the business of destruction. The Book of Wisdom puts it aptly: 'All existing things are dear to you and you hate nothing that you have created – why else would you have made it?' (11:24).

But ... does this mean that God is unconcerned over sin and evil? Surely not. Here our limited human understanding faces a daunting problem. How is one to portray the divinely loving forgiveness of God without conveying the false impression that he shrugs off sin as incidental. The Flood story takes up the challenge. The dramatic significance of the story comes to light in a startling reprise: the repeated statement in the introduction and conclusion of the story. At the beginning: 'every inclination of the thoughts of their hearts was only evil continually' (6:5). At the close, after the promise that there will never be another flood, a similar observation: 'for the inclination of the human heart is evil from youth' (8:21). God has decided to bear with humankind's tendency to evil. One is reminded of Matthew 5:45: 'For the Father makes his sun to rise on the evil and on the good, and sends rain on the righteous and the unrighteous.'

There is our comfort: this foolish God is determined to put up with his wayward children. Edward Schillebeeckx aptly characterises creation, and notably creation of humankind, as a divine adventure full of risks:

> By giving creative space to human beings, God makes himself vulnerable. It is an adventure full of risks ... The creation of human beings is a blank cheque for which God alone is guarantor. By creating human beings with their own finite and free will, God voluntarily renounces power. That makes him to a high degree dependant on human beings and thus vulnerable.[2]

We are reminded of a remarkable episode in Genesis 18. God had decided that he must take action against the wickedness of Sodom and Gomorrah. But he feels he must first brief Abraham: 'Shall I hide from Abraham what I am about to do ... for I have chosen him?' (18:17-19). Abraham, for his part, is flabbergasted. The Lord had not thought the matter through; surely he is not planning to wipe out the righteous! 'Far be it from you to do such a thing, to slay the righteous with the wicked ... shall not

the Judge of all the earth do what is just?' (18:24-26). This is
putting it up to God and no mistake. And, having made his
point, Abraham pleads for the people of Sodom. We catch the
flavour of a bargaining bout in an oriental bazaar with prices
being ruthlessly slashed: 45, 40, 30, 10. He realises that lower
than ten righteous persons he cannot go. But he had had a
valiant try.

That the author of this story could, in such an uninhibited
manner, present this lively dialogue between a human and God,
reveals a profound appreciation of God. He is a transcendent
God, but he is not a remote God. And surely not a fearsome
God. He has a sense of humour. One definition of the human is
animal risibilis – a creature who can laugh. Surely the Creator of
this *animal risibilis* is one who enjoys a joke. He plays along with
Abraham. He is a God who displays respect for humankind.

Sadly, in the Flood story, God had come to observe that the
thoughts and inclinations of humans are perverse. Yet he was
determined that 'never again shall there be a flood to destroy
the earth.' Humankind has not changed. God has changed.
God's purpose had been resisted. His decision is to live with this
resistance. But God is not resigned to evil. He has made a
promise – a covenant: 'I establish my covenant with you, that
never again shall there be a flood to destroy the earth' (9:11).
This is God's own self-limitation on his reaction to sin, to human
spurning of him. The rebellion of humankind had grieved God
to his heart (6:6). God will continue to grieve, will continue to
take the road of suffering:

> God thus determines to take suffering into God's own self
> and bear it there for the future of the world. It is precisely
> this kind of God with whom sinful readers have to do and it
> is primarily the divine commitment to promises made that
> they need most to hear.[3]

God has created humankind in his image. Sinful humans remain in the image of God (9:6), they retain dominion over God's
world. It is, however, a world now touched by their sinfulness
(9:2-3; see Rom 8:18-25). They still have responsibility for the
created order. Humans will continue to fail, but not because creation has failed. And, somehow, God will have the last word.

Lament – Repentance

Humans have to face not alone their sinfulness but also the reality of suffering. One form of response is in prayer – notably prayer of lament and prayer of repentance. Creation faith accepts that God willed to create the world as it is and humans as they are. It accepts without remainder that finitude – contingency – is an inevitable feature of created reality. We are conscious of struggle in our world; we experience suffering within ourselves. The finitude of our world is caught up in God's world of creation. The peril created by these limitations is part and parcel of human existence. It is human destiny to be human beings in a world of failure and suffering. We need to come to terms with suffering as a factor of our experience – of life itself. We need to understand where God fits . And how sufferers relate to God. Here is where lament comes in.

Lament

The language of lament can be uninhibited in the face of suffering that can no longer be comprehended. The accusation is mounted: How could God have allowed this to happen? The accusation is made in the context of talking with God, the context of prayer. It is the very relationship with God that makes the complaint possible. Think of the Cross: My God, my God, why have you forsaken me? It is not at all surprising that lamentation figures largely in the Psalter. Indeed, praise and lament dominate – and the lament is as full a prayer as is the praise.

Psalm 44 is perhaps the most startling text in the Psalter – and the most refreshing! By itself it emphatically confounds a widespread delusion that the God of the Old Testament is One who inspires fear, even dread, a stern God ready to pounce on wrongdoing. The truth is that Israel, with a deep-rooted reverence for God, recognised that God is not mean-minded but is a big God, one who welcomed challenge – witness Moses, or Jeremiah or Job. He could and would take what they might throw at him. This attitude is surely present in Psalm 44, a psalm of lament. For all practical purposes, lament is not currently part of Christian worship. More the pity. Laments pervade the Old Testament – and are not absent from the New. Lament in the Psalter marks only a portion of the whole ambit. Nonetheless, as quite a few people would see it, lament cannot be prayer; it can have no place there. According to this viewpoint, suffering is something to be borne: one 'offers it up'. It is not to be lamented.

Let us be clear: this is emphatically not the view of the people whose faith lies behind the biblical text! In the scriptures that represent their faith and inspire its growth, lamentation reflects the reality of human existence. If pain and suffering are characteristic of human existence (see Genesis 3, for instance), the actual expression of pain is intrinsic to human life: take, for instance, Mark 14:34-36; 15:34 – Gethsemane and the cry from the cross.

There are two kinds of lament: lament for the dead and the lament of affliction. In the Psalter lament of affliction figures as communal lament of the people and as individual lament. In the former, two questions arise: 'Why?' and 'How long?' The question 'Why' asks why has God rejected, abandoned or forgotten his people. The question 'How long?' implies an enduring distress and expresses impatience at the duration. The point is that the accusatory questions are directed at God. Psalm 44 is a dramatic illustration. Psalm 88 is the parade example of individual lament.

Psalm 44
In this communal lament Israel ponders on the seeming absence of Israel's God. First, an ironic *captatio benevolentiae*, a recital of Yahweh's interventions on behalf of the people's ancestors (vv 1-8). 'Our ancestors have told us the story of the things you did in their days, you yourself, in days of long ago.' So far so good … But at verse 9 the psalmist gets down to business. Yes, Yahweh was – at least, so we have been told – a 'great guy' in the past: He is not so hot today! Signs of divine dereliction of duty are glaring. From this verse on, the psalm becomes one long accusation against God. It is all You … You … You … Inexplicably, God has turned against his people:

> You have rejected us … You make us retreat from the foe … You have made us a byword among the nations … You sell your own people for nothing.

This is adding insult to injury – he did not even demand a decent price!

This was the litany of the people's woes. Now the focus switches to the dejected and abandoned people seeking explanation for it all. How could this have befallen us? Israel protests, for a start, that it has not deserved such shabby treatment:

This befell us though we had not forgotten you, though we had not been false to your covenant, though we had not withdrawn our hearts; though our feet had not strayed from your path (vv 17-18).

Worst of all, their God is judged responsible for their distress:

It is from You we face death all day long and are accounted as sheep for the slaughter (v 22).

This aptly sums up the emphasis throughout verses 9-22. God has now to answer for the sorry situation. Then comes the daring challenge of verses 22-26:

Rouse yourself! O Lord, why do you sleep? Why do you hide your face from us?

This is no time for God to sleep. It is high time he recalled his covenant with his people. He is firmly reminded: 'Redeem us for the sake of your steadfast love (covenant love)'.

This is an instance of 'holy blackmail' – and is a recurring motif. The covenant formula is: 'I am your God, you are my people.' The implication here is: We are your people. You seem to have forgotten that you are our God! This is robust prayer indeed. Israel really did have a refreshingly direct approach to its God – perhaps never more so than in prayer.

And yet, although lament is prevalent in the Old Testament, it has not really become part of Christian prayer. Yes, the Psalter is prominent in our worship, and psalms of lament figure largely in the chanting of psalms. The truth, however, is this: the psalms of lament are not acknowledged as such by Christians, for the most part. The Christian who recites a psalm of lament in a formal manner is rarely, if ever, directing a passionate complaint to God – much less at God! We Christians simply manage to miss the point.

So, how has this happened? What lies behind this exclusion of lament (precisely as such) from Christian prayer? Think of it: while the New Testament in no way prevents the Christian from lamenting, in fact the lament (precisely *as* lament) has been excluded in Christian relationship with God, and has virtually disappeared from prayer and worship. This exclusion does not come from the New Testament. It is surely due to Greek influence: the Greek notion of God and the ethic of Stoicism. How different the Hebrew God, who welcomes dialogue and invites plain speaking. Israel obliged!

The fact is, we have tended to become inhibited and 'formulistic' in our prayer. We have imagined there to be an 'appropriate' manner of addressing God – a refined and courtly (and archaic!) language – befitting divinity. We had suffered our 'thees' and 'thous' and 'vouchsafes'. Now, it seems, we have to suffer a new Latinised 'appropriate' prayer language. How sad this is when we consider that we have learned from the Old Testament that God does not ask us to assume a 'proper' and 'godly' style in our prayerful address. We learn that Israel, with a more robust understanding of God, could talk back to him without restraint. It is an approach endorsed by Jesus himself.

Repentance

For the people of Israel, lament was a powerful way of prayer. It was a firm part of their tradition and, because of the prominence of lament in the Psalter, it was an abiding feature of their worship. There is, however, another, a different manner of talking to God. It is one thing to challenge him from the ground of striving to do his will. But when one is conscious of having failed, and failed dismally, what does one do? In this situation we find that post-exilic prayers (prayers in the aftermath of the sixth Babylonian Exile) are encouragement and comfort. In these other prayers the lament element is subdued or absent. They are straightforward: we have sinned; we deserve all that has come upon us. Are we depressed? No! We acknowledge our sin, our shameful ingratitude – and we turn to God. We have sinned, we have failed – but you are You. It is, in some sort, an anticipation of: 'I shall arise and go to my Father.'

Trauma of Exile

> The Lord said to David: 'I will raise up your son after you ...
> and I will establish his kingdom ... your house and your
> kingdom shall be made sure forever before me; your throne
> shall be established forever' (2 Sam 7:12, 16).

What was a native of Judah to think when God's solemn
promise to David had come to nothing? There was no questioning the harsh reality of Nebuchadnezzar's conquest: temple, city
and nation were gone. On the strength of Yahweh's word it
ought not to have been so; but it had happened. For the thought-
ful Yahwist, the disaster was a mirror held up to the nation, a
mirror that showed a visage of gross failure and sin. Some at
least had learned from the bitter experience of the Babylonian
Exile: the faith answer to the disaster was repentance and hope.
The people had failed – of that there could be no doubt. But
Yahweh was steadfast as ever. There was a way of restoration, a
way of redemption. It was the way of candid confession of sin
and of total trust in God's boundless mercy. The many moving
post-exilic prayers to be found in Baruch, Ezra and Nehemiah,
Tobit, Sirach, Esther, Judith and the Book of Daniel follow this
way.[4]

While post-exilic prayers tend to be lengthy, there is about
them a refreshing candour and an inspiring faith. They are the
prayers of a chastened people, a people that, in adversity, had
found its soul. Those who pray confess sin openly. They do not
grovel, but maintain a quiet dignity. Most instructive is a recurring phrase that characterises God as 'the great and awesome
God who keeps covenant and steadfast love with those who
love him and keep his commandments' – followed always by
the confession: 'We have sinned.' Those who pray these prayers
have discovered the way of restoration, the way of redemption.

Daniel
The purpose of the Book of Daniel was to bolster a faith in dan-
ger of being stamped out by the aggression of Antiochus
Epiphanes (175-163 BCE), the Seleucid ruler of Judah. The author
sought to hearten his people and urge them to unyielding loyalty
to their religion. He grounded his summons to courageous faith

on the conviction that God ruled the course of history. Yet, the prayers in the book acknowledge without excuse the failures of Israel and appeal solely to the graciousness of Yahweh. Such is the prayer of Azariah (Dan 3:26-45): 'For you are just in all you have done ... for we have sinned and broken your law in turning away from you; in all matters we have sinned grievously' (3:27-29). Confession of sin is but a prelude to confident hope.

The epitome of these post-exilic prayers is Daniel 9:4-19. This prayer is not only typical, it is the most moving of all these prayers of the chastened. Its conclusion is poignant in its fervour:

> Now therefore, O our God, listen to the prayer of your servant and to his supplication, and for your own sake, Lord, let your face shine upon your desolated sanctuary. Incline your ear, O my God, and hear. Open your eyes and look at our desolation and the city that bears your name. We do not present our supplication before you on the ground of our righteousness but on the ground of your great mercies. O Lord, hear; O Lord, forgive; O Lord, listen and act and do not delay! For your own sake, O my God, because your city and your people bear your name! (9:17-19).

God will respond out of his own mercy alone – 'for your own sake'. And there is that touch of 'holy blackmail', the reminder that the holy city and chosen people are his – bear his name.

There is another prayer, even more eloquent – the apocryphal Prayer of Manasseh. In 2 Kings 21, Manasseh (687-642 BCE) is presented as the most wicked of the kings of Judah. This is repeated in 2 Chronicles 33. The Chronicler, however, tells of Manasseh's conversion and makes reference to his prayer of repentance (2 Chron 33:10-19). Sometime in the first century a Jew, of deep religious sensitivity, decided to give Manasseh his prayer – a sterling example of Jewish piety. The prayer briefly reminds of God's warning to sinners (v 5) and immediately continues:

> Yet immeasurable and unsearchable is your promised mercy,
> for you are the Lord Most High,
> of great compassion,
> long-suffering and very merciful,

and you relent at human suffering.
Lord, according to your great goodness
you have promised repentance and forgiveness
to those who have sinned against you,
and in the multitude of your mercies
you have appointed repentance for sinners.
so that they may be saved (vv 6-7).

The prayer closes on a note of serene confidence:

For you, O Lord, are the God of those who repent,
and in me you will manifest your goodness;
for, unworthy as I am, you will save me
according to your great mercy (vv 13-14).

The point surely is that if even Manasseh (the outstanding biblical sinner) could receive mercy, there is hope for any and every sinner!

God is the Holy One – Holy Mystery. And God is Abba – loving Parent. This God declares: 'I am God and there is no other; I am God and there is no one like me' (Is 46:9). Yet, God speaks to each of us: 'I am your Abba; you are my beloved child.' We know that we are wholly unworthy. But our awareness of unworthiness and sinfulness does not alter the reality. God's love abides, no matter what. Humans have ever found this hard to grasp. Ironically, the staunchly religious have the greater problem. Sinners have an intuitive insight. Jesus' parable of the Pharisee and the Tax Collector (Lk 18:9-14) is apt. The Pharisee 'trusted in himself that he was righteous'; he was comfortable with his God. The sinner was not complacent. He had been branded an outcast, warned that God had no time for him. Yet, his perception, unclouded by an all-too-human image of God, did discern the true God: 'God, be merciful to me, a sinner!' He had the honesty to look at himself, at his sorry state, his radical unworthiness. And he perceived that, notwithstanding, this God loved him.

Paradox of Mercy
When one looks closely at the text of the prophetical books, one observes a striking and consistent factor. Not alone in the

juxtaposition of oracles but, regularly, within an oracle, we find an abrupt change of mood. There is warning and threat, often extensive, to a stubborn and unfaithful people. Then, out of the blue, comes word of salvation. There is no logic to it. That is the beauty of it, and the comfort. There can be no logic because salvation is sheerly grace. God is exuberantly illogical. God's word always is forgiveness. It has to be. He, freely, took the risk of creating humans as free beings. He must, consequently, take responsibility and pay the price. His divine generosity in creation must be matched by the divine generosity of his mercy. A prophetic Paul had glimpsed this. When, at the close of Romans 9-11 he had said goodbye to logic, he could declare not only 'all Israel will be saved' but also, 'For God has imprisoned all in disobedience so that he may be merciful to all' (Rom 11:26, 32). Paul is here in the line of the prophets of Israel. And, of course, in line with the prophet Jesus.

It is not by chance that the prophets, all of them, were poets. Why is it that the prophets have achieved and sustained such influence? It is, in large measure surely, because of the power of their language. The God imaged by them is presented in words that match their poetic insight. In painting divine emotion they play on the gamut of human emotions. And, with poetic abandon, they can present contradictory pictures of God: a God who will not hesitate to punish sinners; a God who has preferential option for sinners. The biblical God is not the immutable, impassible God of our theological tradition. He, along the line of prophetic understanding, is a full-blooded, indeed an earthy God. And never, for a moment, is he any other than God.

Biblical language reminds us that God is not some vague 'force'; God is personal. This language reflects a vitally important perception. The prophets, and biblical writers, were conscious of the transcendence of Yahweh. But they were intensely aware that he was a God close at hand, a God with whom they could and did have dialogue. In speaking of him, and to him, they were prepared to take risks. A striking case in point is the eighth-century prophet Hosea. He was the first to represent the covenant relationship of Yahweh with his people as a marriage. It would have seemed natural enough that the covenant between God and Israel might have been likened to the marriage contract. In practice, it is not the contract aspect that is exploited but, instead, the love aspect and, especially, the love of a husband for his wife. Hosea harked back to the wilderness and the entry into the land. He looked to the graciousness of Yahweh and the rank ingratitude of Israel (Hos 9:10; 11:1-12; 13:4-6). Doubtless, Hosea idealised the wilderness years and painted them as the honeymoon period of God and his people. What matters is that he did not hesitate to cast Yahweh as Spouse of Israel. Bold imagery indeed when the Canaanite religion of Baal was the great challenge: the fertility cult of Baal and his consort Astarte. The prophet knew that, despite the risk of confusion, what mattered was to proclaim the love of God. Theological prudence would not deter him from flaunting his profound conviction. Some might misunderstand – too bad. But those who, like himself, had known the joy and pain of love, would recognise in his long-suffering Spouse their one, true God.

It is clear that the prophets who had, pastorally, to face intransigence from political and religious leaders, and from their own people, retained an insight into divine mercy. Beyond their warnings there is ever a prophetical perception of the profligacy of God. He just will not be confined. His last word simply has to be word of forgiveness.

Hosea
The prophet Hosea bears startling witness:

> She is not my wife, and I am not her husband …
> *Therefore* I will hedge up her way with thorns;
> and I will build a wall against her,
> so that she cannot find her paths …
> *Therefore* I will take back my grain in its time …
> I will punish her for the festival days of the Baals,
> when she offered incense to them …
> and forget me, says the Lord (2:2, 6, 9, 13).

In verses 6 and 9 the 'therefore' (*laken*) introduces, as generally in prophetic texts, a threat (see Amos 3:2; Micah 3:12; Hosea 4:3). The next 'therefore' (v 14) strikes a startlingly different note.

> *Therefore* I will now allure her,
> And bring her into the wilderness, and speak tenderly to her …

There she shall respond as in the days of her youth,
As at the time when she came out of the land of Egypt ...
And I will take you for my wife forever;
I will take you for my wife in righteousness and in justice,
in steadfast love and in mercy.
I will take you for my wife in faithfulness;   '
and you shall know the Lord (2:14-15, 19-20).

In sorrow, Yahweh had divorced his spouse: 'She is not my
wife, and I am not her husband.' Here, as at Babel where his will
to scatter humankind out of his sight (Gen 11:1-9) faltered on his
call of Abraham to a new beginning (12:1-3), and at the Flood
when his grim decision: 'I will blot out from the earth the
human beings I have created ... for I am sorry that I have made
them' flows directly into the declaration: 'But Noah found
favour in the sight of the Lord' (6:7-8), God is inconsistent. Ever,
God's weak side is his love. Divorced Israel may be: the price of
unfaithfulness. In God's eyes, Israel is still his spouse and he
will not give her up.

Jeremiah

A regular assessment of Jeremiah, reflected in the term 'jeremiad'
is not really true to the prophet. Certainly, the Jeremiah of the
book emerges, in the last analysis, as a prophet of hope. The voc-
ational passage (1:4-10) had specified that the message of the
prophet would involve plucking up and destruction but also
building and planting (1:10). The texts of 'building and planting'
are concentrated in chapters 29-33. These chapters are marked
by hope. And here we find the contrast:

For thus says the Lord: your hurt is incurable, your wound is
grievous. There is no medicine for your wound, no healing
for you ... Because your guilt is great, because your sins are
so numerous, I have done these things to you (30:12-13, 15).

The ring of finality seems to exclude all hope. Then, abruptly,
is the assurance:

Therefore all who devour you shall be devoured ...
I will restore health to you and your wounds I will heal, says
the Lord (v 17).

Incurable hurt, no healing available – I will restore health, I will heal! God can do, God will do, what is humanly impossible. He acts in virtue of his infinite love.

Ezekiel

Ezekiel 16:1-52 is the lengthy and consciously crude allegory of the 'brazen whore' Jerusalem.

One must candidly acknowledge that imagery and language are offensive to women. This is a salutary reminder not only that the Bible is an androcentric text but that, until very recently, the whole of theology was firmly male-centred. Granted this, the Ezekiel text is striking. Jerusalem had acted more abominably than her grossly sinful sisters Samaria and Sodom: 'So be ashamed and bear your disgrace, for you have made your sisters appear righteous' (v 52). Then, with startling abruptness, comes v 53: 'I will restore their fortunes, the fortunes of Sodom and her daughters, and I will restore your own fortunes along with theirs.' The passage 16:53-63 is an oracle of restoration:

> I will remember my covenant with you in the days of your youth and I will establish with you an everlasting covenant ... I will establish my covenant with you, and you shall know that I am the Lord ... when I forgive you all you have done, says the Lord God (vv 60, 62-63).

Threat, and seeming rejection, have melted before the fire of love.

Isaiah

The opening and the close of canonical Isaiah aptly illustrate the contrast of threat and salvation:

> Hear, O heavens, and listen, O earth;
> for the Lord has spoken:
> I reared children and brought them up,
> but they have rebelled against me.
> The ox knows its master's crib;
> but Israel does not know,
> my people do not understand (1:2-3).

The Book of Isaiah opens on this note of bewilderment. God is a parent, cut to the quick by the ingratitude of children. That sad ingratitude is documented throughout the chapters of Isaiah. Nevertheless we have, in the meantime, been so well prepared that we have come to take for granted the tone of the closing chapter:

> Rejoice with Jerusalem, and be glad for her,
> all you who love her;
> rejoice with her in joy,
> all you who mourn over her –
> that you may nurse and be satisfied
> with her consoling breast;
> that you may drink deeply with delight
> from her glorious bosom.
> For thus says the Lord:
> I will extend prosperity to her like a river,
> and the wealth of the nations like an overflowing stream;
> and you shall nurse and be carried on her arm,
> and dandled on her knees.
> As a mother comforts her child,
> so I will comfort you;
> you shall be comforted in Jerusalem (66:10-13).

Here, God's children nurse at the breast of Jerusalem – a lovely image of peace and contentment. Striking is the switch in v 13 to the motherhood of God. In Ezekiel 34, God had had enough of alleged shepherds; he decided to take personal charge. We get a similar picture here with God becoming a nursing mother.

What has been offered above is a very confined cross-section, no more than that. The remarkable fluctuation we have noted in the prophets can be documented over and over. It is not rarity; it is the norm.[5] And the flow is always in the same direction: threat is followed by word of hope and salvation. The pattern surely means that God's final word is mercy and forgiveness. And this feature is to be found not only in the prophets. The God of the Bible, the Father of our Lord Jesus Christ, is the foolish God (see 1 Corinthians 1:18-21).

Merciful to All

Our God, who spoke the first creative word is determined to
have the last word. This, of course, is as it should be. That word
has to be good news. What we have perceived of the sheer graciousness of God would urge us to see it so. Israel, notably in
prayer of lament, had discerned this. There is robust faith and
firm hope in the plaintive 'Why?' and 'How long?' There is a
holy impatience to it. It springs from the conviction that God can
do better, much better, than he is doing. There is nothing mean-
spirited in the repentance of Israel. Confession of sin carries the
assurance that sin has been forgiven. The prophets have consist-
ently perceived word of mercy behind warning and threat – beyond even divine chastisement as they reckoned it. The question, then, arises: Will God's word of mercy eventually embrace
all of humankind? A vital factor here is human freedom and
God's utter respect of our freedom. Precisely because of the freedom factor it is impossible to say, definitively, that salvation
will be universal. But, when one focuses on God, then one may
appropriately hope for the salvation of the whole human race. It
is not a vain hope. It carries an impressive scriptural warranty.

Salvation

What is salvation? It is perceived in various ways; it has been
made to mean many things. It has been made to seem ethereal,
unreal. It has been presented as transcending humanness, even
as denying humanness. This is tragic because salvation means
nothing other than attaining perfect humanness. We are human
beings, created in the image of God; we are meant to image God.
Our destiny is to be human – as God understands humanness.
We are meant to be human beings in a sphere that is, simply, the
world. It is futile to look for salvation beyond our creaturely existence. As Edward Schillebeeckx puts it:

> The world and the human history in which God wills to
> bring about salvation for men and women are the basis of the
> whole reality of salvation: there salvation is achieved in the
> first instance … In this sense, it is true that there is no salv-
> ation, not even any religious salvation, outside the human
> world.[6]

Salvation is salvation of and for human beings – men and women of flesh and blood. Salvation is not, nor was it ever meant to be, salvation of 'souls'.[7] It includes and involves society and the world of nature. It comprises eschatological, social and political aspects. 'Belief in God is a belief in God's absolute saving presence among men and women in their history ... There is no situation in which God cannot be near to us and in which we cannot find him.'[8] Salvation has been understood – or misunderstood – in so many ways. It surely cannot mean being shielded from our finitude and everything that this finitude involves. The process of salvation means that, here and now, we strive to be human – in our mortality and in our suffering. If this is not so, then Jesus of Nazareth is not the whole human being that our faith acknowledges him to be. Ultimately, salvation reaches to human existence beyond death.

Universal Salvation
If salvation means fellowship with God and blessedness of eternal life with God, universal salvation means that all human beings will eventually be redeemed by God's gracious love – a love displayed ultimately in Jesus Christ. On the other hand, a limited salvation view assumes that only those who, in this life, acknowledge the true God and, in the Christian setting, confess Christ as Lord, will finally be saved. Both views – limited salvation and universal salvation – are found prominently in both Old Testament and New Testament. A stream of texts maintains that final salvation is limited (e.g. Is 26:20-21; 66:15-16; Mt 25:31-46; Jn 3:36). Another stream suggests or affirms universal salvation (e.g. Is 66:18-23; Jn 3:17; Rom 11:32-36; 1 Tim 2:3-4). Here it will suffice to list some further texts that point firmly towards universal salvation: Psalm 86:9; Isaiah 25:6, 8; 52:10; John 12:23; 1 Corinthians 15:22, 28; Philippians 2:10-11; 1 Timothy 2:3-4; 4:10; Titus 2:11. Somewhat surprisingly, this view is present throughout the Book of Revelation: 1:7; 5:13; 14:6-7; 15:3-4; 21:3, 24-27.[9]

Arguably, the weightiest text in favour of universal salvation is found in Paul. In Romans 9-11 he addresses the problem: How could God's people have failed to recognise God's final Messenger? Throughout the chapters he wrestled with a humanly incomprehensible situation but never loosed his grip on his conviction of God's utter faithfulness: '... the gifts and calling of God are irrevocable' (11:29). At the end, he committed the whole matter to God and declared, in words that had little to do with the forced logic of his argument up to now: 'And so all Israel will be saved ... (11:26). A remarkable statement. Then Paul took a truly giant step: 'For God has imprisoned all in disobedience so that he may be merciful to all' (11:32). His declaration has to be seen in contrast to the unrelieved picture he had painted in Romans 1-3: All humanity stands under sin, cut off from God. But, then, that backdrop was designed to highlight the incredible graciousness of God.[10]

The judgement scene in Revelation 20:11-15 is enlightening. There, in the presence of the One on a great white throne, all are assembled for judgement. 'Books were opened. Also another book was opened, the book of life. And the dead were judged according to their works, as recorded in the books' (v 12). People are judged by what they had done, or had failed to do. There is human responsibility. Yet, what is ultimately decisive is whether one's name is inscribed in the book of life. We write the 'books'; God writes the 'Book'. Salvation is God's prerogative. Salvation is grace: gift, pure and simple. God's word of judgement is word of graciousness.

God's saving purpose for humanity – the *Eschaton* , the End – is salvation, There is no negative eschaton: God does not will damnation.[11] For that matter, 'positive eschaton only' might be a better way of stating what 'universal salvation' is meant to express. Salvation is offered to all. But God is God of freedom; he will not compel. Whether any person, faced with Infinite Love, can choose to embrace evil – and, at some point, the choice must be stark; anything less would be unworthy of our God – we do not know. What must surely follow from the character of our God is this: There is one way and one way only in which a human person may not be saved. That is by cold-blooded rejection of a *Parent* who is sheer *Love*. One leaves salvation firmly where it belongs. God and Lamb alone know what names are inscribed in the book of life (see Rev 20:11-15; 17:8). And, appreciating something of the foolishness of our God, one rather suspects that the names of all humans will be read in that Book.

CHAPTER FIVE

Love

You are precious in my sight, and honoured, and I love you.
(Isaiah 43:4)

One might say that this chapter had been written already, in what has come before. The Bible is nothing other than the turbulent love-story of God and humankind. *This Tremendous Lover* is the title of a book on prayer by the Irish Cistercian Eugene Boylan – an inspired title which aptly describes our God. *This Tremendous Lover* – too big for our pettiness. We are adept at cutting God to our measure. Happily, our paper-patterns will never translate into anything real. God, gently or painfully, sets our ways aside. Why, then, does he let us hurt ourselves and hurt one another so? We need to understand that God, our Parent, has infinite respect for us. God is God of power, omnipotent – but never a God of force. His respect for his creatures, above all for his human creatures, is divine. He invites us, longingly, lovingly, to respect one another. The temptation is to look through our human chaos to an uncaring God. The challenge is to find, in our troubled world, the presence of a loving God. If true love respects the one loved, what may we expect from a loving God? One needs humility (another word for honesty) to learn the reality of love.

It is a wondrous and humbling thought that God has such respect for us. If we would grasp this truth, so much would hang together. There is, in all of us, something of the impatience of the Pharisees who sought a sign from heaven (Mk 8:11). We will not be content with the human way. Someone has said that the secret of holiness is the doing of ordinary things extraordinarily well. Jesus went about 'doing good'. There is little doubt that his way was far less marked by the miraculous than the gospels would suggest. We have come to realise the extent to which the Jesus-story has been coloured by Easter faith. In the light of their encounter with the risen Lord, there is no way the disciples would ever again think of Jesus only as they had known him before his death. What is encouraging is that the pre-Easter Jesus of Nazareth is still accessible to us.

Parent and Children

God, we have seen, is the Holy One – Holy Mystery. And God is Abba – loving Parent. This God declares: 'I am God and there is no other; I am God and there is no one like me' (Is 46:9). Yet, God speaks to each of us: I am your Abba; you are my beloved child. We know that we are wholly unworthy. But our awareness of unworthiness and sinfulness does not alter the reality. God's love abides, no matter what. Humans have ever found this hard to grasp. Ironically, the staunchly religious have the greater problem. Sinners have an intuitive insight. Jesus' parable of the Pharisee and the Tax Collector (Lk 18:9-14) is apt. The Pharisee 'trusted in himself that he was righteous'; he was comfortable with his God. The sinner was not complacent. He had been branded an outcast, warned that God had no time for him. Yet, his perception, unclouded by an all-too-human image of God, did discern the true God: 'God, be merciful to me, a sinner!' He had the honesty to look at himself, at his sorry state, his radical unworthiness. And he perceived that, notwithstanding, this God loved him.

Graciousness

Nothing escapes the eye of God. How regularly this observation has been cast as sanction, as threat. God does indeed keep a close eye on us – but to acknowledge whatever good we do (see Mt 6:4, 6, 18; 10:42). Our good works carry no price tag; there is no 'merit' in that sense. What is so much more important is 'recompense': gracious acknowledgment by a gracious God. To his eye, nothing of good we do is unobserved or unimportant. Not surprisingly because, wherever there is good, it is of God. There are many, very many, who feel that they do not know God, yet, in fact, who witness to him – by doing good. They may not know God, but God knows them, and rejoices in them.

For one who claims to know God, it is vitally important that one know and acknowledge the true God. When I have come to know, to experience, the graciousness of God, I will not only readily discern but firmly reject anything and everything that would temper or cloud this graciousness. This asks of me that I dare to acknowledge my God of infinite love and mercy and forgiveness. I recall an observation of C. H. Dodd in his classic commentary on Romans:

> The author of Hebrews has said, 'It is an awful thing to fall into the hands of the living God.' Paul, with a finer instinct, has seen that the really awful thing is to fall out of his hands.[1]

I grow more sure of the wisdom of that remark. The comfort is that, once within the shelter of God's hands, it is not at all easy to fall out of them. But one must recognise the shelter.

'Long ago God spoke to our ancestors in many and various ways by the prophets, but in these last days he has spoken to us by a Son' (Heb 1:1-2). God had spoken indeed, and we have noted something of the graciousness of his word. The promise in his words of the past has found fulfilment in the Word who is the Son. The human race stands in need of redemption. God took the initiative. He laid claim on us and has given us a claim on him. He is God for us – the living God who created us and called us to be his daughters and his sons. 'For God so loved the world that he gave his only Son' (Jn 3:16). The giving of the Son shows beyond doubt that God is in deadly earnest. God is ever Father of the 'prodigal son', who looks eagerly for the homecoming of the child, who is ready to take off and embrace him fondly when he appears on the horizon. Thanks to the foolishness of God, reconciliation is not our task or achievement. It is the gift of a loving Parent.

Paul had understood that 'God was in Christ, reconciling the world to himself' (2 Cor 5:19). 'Reconciliation' is the keyword. Throughout the Bible rings the anguished cry of humankind gone astray. And it is only too humanly understandable that there should be a frantic scramble to effect reconciliation with God – through cult and ritual, through scrupulous observance of law. Always there was the more enlightened recognition that reconciliation was God's deed. So, for instance, Lamentations 5:21: 'Restore us to yourself, O Lord, that we may be restored.' Paul is following a thoroughly Jewish tradition when he insists on this. He had come to understand that God had ever longed to reconcile humanity to himself. Reconciliation is God's deed, not ours. The answer to the perennial temptation to be like God is to let God *be* God in one's life.

There is our hope, a hope that rests upon the love of God shown in the gift of the Son on our behalf while we were sinners. Now that we are God's friends, that hope must surely see us through to the end (see Rom 5:6-10; 8:32). That hope is a challenge to live out the fact of righteousness, of being set right with God by God, to reach the goal of salvation. The basis of hope is firm indeed: 'God proves his love for us in that while we were sinners Christ died for us' (5:8). We were 'sinners' – weak, without moral capacity. Christ died to rescue us from that state. This showed, unmistakably, God's personal love for us. Christ's self-gift in love is the historical expression of the eternal love of God. It is a love that knows no limit because it is the love of the God who 'justifies the ungodly' (4:5) – those alienated from God. More simply, God is the Judge who acquits the guilty. This paradox challenges the propriety of imaging or speaking of God as Judge at all. Simply, God is Love.

In our world, however, salvation is still a matter of hope. We may believe that, in principle, salvation has been achieved. Our experience, personal and of our world, constantly reminds us that, in practice, much is unredeemed. One listens to Paul:

> We know that the whole creation has been groaning in labour pains until now; and not only creation, but we ourselves, who have the first fruits of the Spirit, groan inwardly while we wait for adoption, the redemption of our bodies. For in hope we were saved (Rom 8:22-27).

The Riddle of Suffering

There are experiences common to all human beings such as the experience of birth and death – and the experience of suffering. We humans are so fragile, so vulnerable. We are open to disease that may touch us even before birth. Pain and suffering, to a lesser or greater extent, are part of our human lot. But let us be honest about it, a frightening share of human suffering is wrought by humans. Man's inhumanity to man is the great sin, the challenge to God's loving purpose for his children. I have

used man in a generic sense. Taken in a gender sense, man's inhumanity to woman, rampant in many cultures, and serious in
ours, is obscene perversion of God's purpose. We bring much
pain upon ourselves and upon others.

There remains the suffering that is not of our causing. Herein
lie both riddle and scandal. Suffering that has a human source
we can understand – though we still ask: Why? Suffering that
seems to come, in some fashion, from our God – that is pro-
foundly disturbing. Must our suffering be ascribed to an al-
legedly beneficent God? Early Israel could simply answer: Yes,
God is author of suffering. Later Israel modified this view. The
Christian must repudiate it. But, then, the problem of innocent
suffering becomes more, not less, acute. It is not a new problem.
It is obvious that the first Christians were embarrassed by the
suffering and death of Jesus – the Messiah. They solved the
problem in terms of enigmatic divine purpose:

> '… this man, handed over to you according to the definite
> plan and foreknowledge of God, you crucified and killed'
> (Acts 2:23).

We should be clear, however, that the 'definite plan and foreknowledge of God' does not envisage an inflexible divine strategy.
It is, in fact, a manner of saying: We do not know why the Son,
the sinless one, had to suffer and to die. God knows. Jesus laid
down his life in loving response to the Father's love – love of the
Son and of humanity. The Father did not demand the death of
Jesus. The Father did not seek the death of Jesus: 'Surely they
will respect my Son' (Mk 12:6 and parallel texts). The Father
gave his Son for humankind – and gave him *eis telos*, in boundless love. God would show human beings that his love for them
was in deadly earnest. The Father did not bring about the death
of the Son – Jesus died at the hands of his religious and political
enemies. But the Father did not shrink from having him 'delivered up' to his enemies. Only so does the death of Jesus fall
within the 'definite plan and foreknowledge of God'. And, in
filial acceptance of God's saving purpose, and only so, did Jesus
accept death. He was obedient unto death – with an obedience
that was a loving yes to a purpose of sheerest love. 'God so
loved the world …' There is no gainsaying that word. It is the

only explanation of the death of Jesus that is consonant with the character of our God.

As regards innocent suffering in general, the answer lies in faith. We Christians must emulate the faith of the mighty Job who, when faced with the arbitrariness of his God, clung to his faith in the merciful God of his previous experience. Faith does not call for a suspension of reason. It assures us, instead, that God is greater than our reasoning. Unmerited suffering, innocent suffering – that is wrong, that is scandal. Our God is not unmindful of the scandal. His Son, the sinless one, suffered. We Christians must leave the mystery of suffering in the hands of God, trusting that his love has the answer to the riddle. This is not to say that we do not strive to understand it as best we may. At least we can unburden ourselves of misunderstanding. And we have the right to lament, to cry out to God, the right to ask 'Why?' and 'How long?'

Forgiveness

Forgiveness does not come lightly. An offence is all the more hurtful when it is inflicted by one near and dear. In our human way we think it reasonable that forgiveness be shrouded in conditions; we exact reparation of some sort. This is not to suggest that forgiveness may not be wholehearted and sincere. And there is the fact that, humanly speaking, and with the best intention, it is simply not easy to forget a deep hurt. The reminder of it is within us, in our very being.

One of the things about God which humans find hard to accept is the breadth and depth of his forgiveness. When we temper the forgiveness of God by the standard of our forgiveness, we get it wrong. And we have, unhappily, tended to imagine divine forgiveness in terms of a human model. Indeed, consistent with our flawed image of God, we assume that such forgiveness is grudging: an offended deity is prepared to forgive, provided he gets his pound of flesh. It is a sad travesty of God's forgiveness. Yet it is one that is prevalent.

The robust faith of the prophets may bring encouragement. Isaiah carries a prayer attributed to King Hezekiah after he had been snatched from the brink of death. It has the hopeful word: 'It was for my welfare that I had great bitterness ... for you have

cast all my sins behind your back' (Is 38:17). Micah, in his lament
for Zion, declares:

> Who is a God like you, pardoning iniquity, and passing over
> transgressions? ... He will again have compassion upon us,
> he will tread our iniquities under foot. You will cast all our
> sins into the depths of the sea (Mic 7:18-19).

What powerful images! What mighty consolation. 'You have
cast all my sins behind your back': you have snatched them
from me, you have cast them behind, thrown them over your
shoulder, and have walked on, without a backward glance. 'He
will tread our iniquities under foot': he will cover them over
deeply and firmly, will bury them forever from his sight. 'You
will cast all my sins into the depths of the sea': you will lift the
crushing burden that wears us down and sink them in the
murky depths where such dark things belong.

This is the prophets' image of divine forgiveness, worthy of
their God. Only Jesus could do better with his unforgettable picture of the loving Father who, without question and without
condition, welcomes and reinstates his errant son (Lk 15:20-24).
We who are so generous in depicting the stern justice of God are
so miserly in painting his love and mercy. It seems that we cannot abide a God who is more truly human than we.[2]

CHAPTER SIX

God with us

No one has ever seen God; the only Son, who is close to the
Father's heart, he has made him known (John 1:18).

The God who did not will to be alone created humankind.
Loving Parent, he constantly called out: 'Here am I, here am I'
(Is 65:1). He waited for a response, waited not only in patience
but with divine compassion. And, from that human race, in
God's good time, issued the one who responded, wholly. In
him, the perfect response to God, God could be, God would be,
God in history. God could, God now would, enter wholly into
human joy and human sorrow. God would have, to the full,
compassion with women and men in their pain and in their
death. It was his purpose from the start. 'God remembered
Noah' (Gen 8:1): he would henceforth bear with humankind.
'The Lord said to Abram (12:1): he launched his plan to save humankind. 'He did not spare his own Son' (Rom 8:32): God
showed that he really is God *for us*.

Who, then, is God? Our God is Father of our Lord Jesus
Christ who has shown himself in the life and cross of Jesus. God
is truly the God of the Old Testament whom Jesus addressed as
Abba. The difference is that, through revelation by the Son, we
see God more clearly. The New Testament brings more sharply
and emphatically before us a concerned and caring Parent: 'God
so loved the world that he gave his only Son' (Jn 3:16). God is the
Father who has given us the Son – given us himself. We measure
love by our experience of love. When we strive to measure divine love we need to think the unthinkable, believe the unbe-
lievable. God has revealed himself to us in the human person, in
the life, death and resurrection of Jesus of Nazareth. In him, God
has come to walk with us. In him God has suffered among us
and at our hands. It is always the same God, the one God, from
the first page of the Bible to the last.

Jesus of Nazareth

'Let us run with perseverance the race that is set before us, look-
ing to Jesus the pioneer and perfecter of our faith' (Heb 12:1-2).
For the author of Hebrews, faith in Jesus, the high priest seated
'at the right hand of the throne of God' (12:12), is what gives
meaning to the Christian way. At the same time, no other New
Testament writer has stressed more than he the humanity of this
heavenly high priest – for he has in sight a specific historical person: Jesus of Nazareth.

Yet, after New Testament times, what came to be was ahist-
orical christology that displayed little of the vulnerable Jesus
who died on a cross. Even when they have kept the earthly Jesus
in view, people have tended to detach the death of Jesus from
his life and his resurrection from his career and death. To do this
is to ignore the challenge of the prophet Jesus and, ultimately, to
fail to grasp the significance of his death and the true meaning of
his resurrection. The life of Jesus of Nazareth is the key to what
Christianity is all about. In the human Jesus we meet God. This
is the astounding truth at the heart of Christianity.

Image of the Invisible God

'Who do you say that I am?' (Mk 8:29). This challenging question
put to the disciples at Caesarea Philippi is one that Christians
have continued to face over the centuries. It might be argued
that the earliest answers are still the best. One looks to Paul. His
response rings with conviction: Jesus 'is the image of the invisible God' (Col 1:15). The Fourth Gospel offers a relevant
commentary: 'No one has ever seen God; the only Son, who is
close to the Father's heart, who has made him known' (Jn 1:18).
The transcendent, incomprehensible God is now visible and
knowable in the incarnate Son – and only in him: 'the Word became flesh and lived among us' (1:14). And, throughout the
Fourth Gospel, the role of the Son is Revealer of the Father. The
author of Hebrews makes his contribution:

> Long ago God spoke to our ancestors in many and various
> ways by the prophets, but in these last days he has spoken to
> us by a Son … He is the reflection of God's glory and the
> exact imprint of God's very being (1:1-3).

God had indeed spoken in the scriptures of Israel, and continues to speak to us there. But there is now, besides, a definitive word, a word not uttered or written, a word that is person, the Son. And this person, who reflects God's glory and carries the imprint of the very reality of God, 'had to be like his brothers and sisters in every respect ... tested as we are', sharing 'our flesh and blood' (2:17; 4:15; 2:14). Jesus is divine indeed, with a divinity that finds whole expression in a full humanity. Put more simply, Jesus is the human person in whom God is wholly present.

If Jesus bears the stamp of God's very being, he does so as a human person, like us in all things. Jesus tells us what God is like, Jesus is God's summons to us, God's challenge to us. In Jesus God has shown himself in human form – 'he is the image of the invisible God' (Col 1:15). In practice, we have slipped quickly past this human aspect. We have turned instead to a 'divine icon' comfortably free of any trait of the critical prophet. We have consigned Jesus to his heavenly home – and wisely, because we realised a long time ago that he is safer there! We genuflect before 'our divine Lord' who does not impinge on us because of how we envisage him. He really has no critical impact on the life of our world. But Jesus of Nazareth is a very uncomfortable person to have about. The gospel stands, and its challenge, its 'dangerous memory'.

The mystery of Jesus is that, in him, God communicates himself in a full and unrestricted manner: 'In him all the fulness of God was pleased to dwell' (Col 1:19). Jesus' divinity is not, as sometimes presented, a sort of second substance in him. His divinity lies in the fact that, as the perfect counterpart of God, he is the manifestation and presence of God in our world. When the human Jesus is not acknowledged, our understanding of God suffers:

> The gospel is good news not just about Jesus but about the God of Jesus, the maker of heaven and earth, the God of all men and women ... We Christians learn to express stammeringly the content of what "God" is and the content of what humanity can be, from the career of Jesus.[1]

Defining God

> Now after John was arrested [delivered up] Jesus came to
> Galilee proclaiming the good news of God, and saying, 'The
> time is fulfilled, and the kingdom of God has come near; re-
> pent and believe in the good news' (Mark 1:14-15).

Jesus is here firmly cast as a prophet, issuing a challenge and
an invitation. He had a burning desire for the renewal of the
people of Israel as God's holy elect. He would not define the
holiness of God's people in cultic terms. He redefined it in terms
of wholeness. Where other contemporary Jewish movements
were, in their various ways, exclusive, the Jesus movement was
inclusive. His challenge and his invitation were to all. What
Jesus claimed was that the intervention of God expected for the
End-time was, in some sort, happening in his ministry. The
kingdom is, here and now, present in history in that the power
of evil is broken, sins are forgiven, sinners are gathered into
God's friendship. The kingdom, though in its fullness still in the
future, comes as present offer, in actual gift, through the proclamation of the good news. But it arrives only on condition of the
positive response of the hearer.

The Rule of God
The phrase 'kingdom of God' occurs only once in the Old
Testament, in Wisdom 10:10. The expression was not current in
Judaism at the time of Jesus and was not widely used by early
Christians. 'Kingdom of God' is found predominantly in the
synoptic gospels and then almost always on the lips of Jesus. It
was evidently central to Jesus' proclamation. It was his way of
speaking of God himself coming in power to manifest his definitive rule in the end-time. This is why 'reign' or 'rule' of God is a
more satisfactory rendering of the Aramaic *malkutha di elaha*,
which would have been Jesus' term. Jesus preached the kingdom: he proclaimed that God is the ultimate meaning of the
world. The rule of God does not signify something 'spiritual',
outside of this world. Jesus was supremely concerned with our
real world. He spoke so vaguely of the future that the first
Christians could expect that the end would come in their day
(see 1 Thess 4:15, 17; Mk 9:1; 13:20). When he preached the king-

dom of God, he envisaged a revolution in the existing order. He made two fundamental demands: he asked for personal conversion and he postulated a restructuring of the human world. Conversion (*metanoia*) meant changing one's mode of thinking and acting to suit God's purpose for humankind. It would be a new manner of existing before God.

But conversion also meant a turning from the established order. Jesus made the point, so clearly and effectively developed by Paul, that it is not law that saves – not even the Law – it is love. Jesus' outlook and conduct were marked by freedom. His understanding of freedom is again faithfully reflected by Paul: freedom to serve. Jesus did not make life easier. His disconcerting word was that love knows no limits. He proclaimed not law but good news. The gospel is good news for one who can grasp its spirit and react positively to it. His good news embraced basic equality: all men and women, as children of the Father, are brothers and sisters. Good news so understood is a radical challenge to all social and ecclesiastical systems based on power. Edward Schillebeeckx has expressed this forcefully:

> 'Kingdom of God', a key term in the message of Jesus, is the biblical expression for the nature of God – unconditional and liberating sovereign love – in so far as this comes to fruition in the lives of men and women who do God's will, and is manifested in them. The kingdom of God is a new relationship of human beings to God, with as its tangible and visible side a new type of liberating relationship between men and women, within a peaceful reconciled society ... The kingdom of God is a new world of suffering removed, as world of completely whole or healed men and women in a society where master-servant relationships no longer prevail, quite different from life under Roman occupation. Precisely at this point Jesus turns especially to the poor ... Jesus was aware that he was acting as God would do. He translates God's action for men and women ... To act as Jesus does is praxis of the kingdom of God and also shows what the kingdom of God is: salvation for men and women.[2]

Salvation

Sinful humanity stands in need of salvation. Salvation is God's deed. All have sinned. All 'are now justified by his grace as a gift, through the redemption that is in Christ Jesus, whom God put forward as a means of expiation (*hilasterion*) by his blood, effective through faith' (Rom 3:24-25). In Greek, the root-verb of the noun *hilasterion* has two meanings: 'to placate' a man or a god'; 'to expiate' a sin. In the Septuagint (the Greek Old Testament) the first meaning is not used in reference to God while the other meaning is frequent. There can be no doubt at all that for Paul the noun means 'an act by which guilt is removed'. He is declaring that Christ's death is the means by which God forgives sins.

Paul had spent most of the first three chapters of Romans presenting in the starkest terms the plight of humankind before the coming of Christ. It is the backdrop to his picture of God's incredible love towards sinful humanity (chaps 5-8). 'God shows his love for us in that while we were yet sinners Christ died for us' (5:8) – for the 'ungodly' (v 6), the estranged from God. Paul goes on to describe the deed of God as reconciliation: 'we were reconciled … we have received our reconciliation' (5:10-11). We have noted that *hilasterion*, in Paul's usage, cannot possibly mean the placating of an angry God. If there were any doubt it must be laid now. It could not be clearer that it is not God who is the one reconciled. We are reconciled to God by God: it is he who does the reconciling. 'God was in Christ, reconciling the world to himself' (2 Cor 5:19). God is the *subject* of reconciliation, the one who does it – never the *object*. One wonders how theories of satisfaction and propitiation could ever have been constructed and, more disturbingly, how they have prevailed.[3]

'God was in Christ, reconciling the world to himself.' This is arguably the very best christological statement, and it weds christology with soteriology. Where Jesus is, there is God; and God is God for us. God reconciles to himself through Christ. God reconciles by making God's own self the site of reconciliation. Christ Jesus was the means of reconciliation – by his 'blood', his death. As the Suffering Servant, 'he was wounded for our transgressions, crushed for our iniquities … the Lord has laid on him the iniquity of us all' (Is 53:5-6). In the person of the Son, God took upon himself all the suffering of the world, all the sin of the world and, by absorbing it, put it out of commission. Evil can ultimately be overcome only by love.

> The cross is part of the way of salvation. Yet the cross does not or should not exalt suffering or image God as vengeful, angry, unmerciful, or unforgiving. The cross is redemptive because it is the transforming identification of God with all who are desperate, oppressed, or guilty, signaling the raising of all into divine love. The cross saves within a process of incarnation, resurrection, and the sending of Christ's Spirit.[4]

'I, when I am lifted up from the earth, will draw all to myself' (Jn 12:32). Lifted up on the cross, Jesus drew into himself all the suffering of the world. He can gather to himself, and to God, a humanity now set free from its burden of sin. The author of Hebrews finds the meaning of the life of Jesus in his crucifixion – accepted as a self-sacrifice for broken humanity. He had come to do the saving will of the Father and he had learned God's purpose in the 'school of suffering' (Heb 5:8). In Gethsemane he had prayed 'with loud cries and tears to the one who was able to save him from death' (5:7). He came to understand that the way of faithfulness led to the cross.

The sacrifice of Jesus did not end on the cross. By God's graciousness (Heb 2:9) his death was for the benefit of all men and women. The Father had seen in the death of Jesus the supreme assertion of his love for humankind and his faithfulness toward God – for we must always have in mind that the meaning of Jesus' death is to be found in his life. Exaltation to the right hand of the Father is the divine acknowledgment of the significance of the death of Jesus, giving this death its abiding, eternal value.

God is revealed with unwonted clarity in one human life and in one episode of human history. If Jesus is the image of the invisible God, the cross is the revelation of true God and true humanness. On the cross Jesus shows what it is to be human. God's Son dramatically demonstrates the radical powerlessness of the human being. He shows that we are truly human when we accept our humanity, when we face the fact that we are not masters of our fate. The cross offers the authentic definition of what it is to be human: God's definition. There he starkly and firmly reminds us of who and what we are.[5]

In the cross God defined the human being as creature – not to crush or humiliate, but that he might be, as Creator, wholly with his creature – to be Parent, with his child. On its own, humankind has indeed reason to fear. In God, in total dependence on God, there is no place for fear. The resurrection of Jesus makes that clear, for the raising of Jesus from death is God's endorsement of the definition of God established on the cross. It is there he defines himself against all human caricatures of him. God, in the cross, is a radical challenge to our hubris, our pride. He is the God who has entered, wholly, into rejection and humiliation. He is the God present in human life where to human eyes he is absent. He is God of humankind. He is God for us – all because he has made his self known to us in the Son who is 'like us in all things.'

The Way

We cannot but believe that the first Christians had an understanding of Jesus sharpened by their very nearness to 'the things that have happened in these days ... concerning Jesus of Nazareth' (Lk 24:18-19) – an understanding that, for us, has been blunted by a weight of theology – not always helpful. It is not easy for us to fight our way through to Jesus of Nazareth. It is essential that we strive.

We do want to make our way to God. What we must learn to accept is that God has first made his way to us! The first sin was humanity's snatching at the wisdom that could only be theirs as gift (Gen 3:1-7). Humanity's sin continues to be its striving to escape the ways of God. It has long perturbed me that Old Testament men and women often had a better understanding of God and, certainly, a more personal relationship with God than is the experience of many Christians. In Jesus of Nazareth the divine has entered into our world, our history. God has become one with us. But we would bypass the way of God. That primal temptation is still there: 'You will be like God.' The basic Christian truth is: 'I am the Way' (Jn 14:6). If God's way to humankind is through the man Jesus, then our way to God is through the man Jesus.

I have stressed the *man* Jesus – is Jesus not God? I would sug-gest that the statement 'Jesus is God' is not only not a criterion of orthodoxy; I would argue that it effectively blunts the challenge of Jesus. A Jesus who is 'God' is a Jesus we can manipulate – we can make anything we please of 'God'. Besides, to say 'Jesus is God' implies not only that we know who Jesus is – but that we know who and what God is. This observation of Albert Nolan is salutary:

> By his words and his praxis, Jesus himself changed the con-tent of the word 'God'. If we do not allow him to change our image of God, we will not be able to say that he is our Lord and God. To choose him as our God is to make him the source of our information about divinity and to refuse to superimpose upon him our own ideas of divinity.
>
> This is the meaning of the traditional assertion that Jesus is the Word of God. Jesus reveals God to us, God does not re-veal Jesus to us. God is not the Word of Jesus, that is to say, our ideas about God cannot throw any light upon the life of Jesus. To argue from God to Jesus instead of arguing from Jesus to God is to put the cart before the horse. This, of course, is what many Christians have tried to do. It has gen-erally led them into a series of meaningless speculations which only cloud the issue and which prevent Jesus from re-vealing God to us.[6]

Jesus, the man of flesh and blood, we cannot manipulate. And he shows us the true image of God whom we find to be, paradoxically, a *Deus humanissimus* – a supremely human God – this Father of our Lord Jesus Christ. But we can see him only if we allow Jesus of Nazareth to be human. This Jesus is, indeed, Emmanuel, he is God-with-us. We are faced with mystery here. How is one to speak of this unique meeting of God with human-ity, this union of divinity and humanness, in terms that will not betray one or the other aspect of the mystery? For my part, I am not prepared to sacrifice Jesus' humanness to a misguided con-cern to 'rescue' his divinity.

Paul has assured us that 'God was in Christ, reconciling the world to himself' (2 Cor 5:19). My God, then, is a God bent on humankind. My God is a God who so loves the world that he gave his Son. My God acknowledges the worship of him in his childrens' caring for one another. That is what the great prophets of Israel saw and proclaimed. That is the way and the message of Jesus of Nazareth. But we do not like to be told that the meeting-place with God is the sacrament of my brother and sister. Will the elder son in the parable of the Prodigal Son acknowledge his brother and enter into the joy of his homecoming (Lk 15:25-32)? Only so can he know his Father. We may ignore, but we cannot deny, that such is the praxis and the teaching of Jesus (see Mt 25:31-46). He is Revealer of God – our Parent.

Father – Son – Spirit

Jesus proclaimed:
> Let anyone who is thirsty come to me,
> and let the one who believes in me drink.

As the scripture has said:
> 'Out of his heart shall flow rivers of living water.'
> Now this he said about the Spirit …
> for as yet the Spirit had not been given
> because Jesus was not yet glorified (Jn 7:37-9).

> When Jesus had received the wine, he said, 'It is finished';
> and he bowed his head and handed over the Spirit (Jn 19:30).

In Jn 7:37-39 Jesus promised that when he was 'glorified' – fully manifested by his death on the cross – those who believed in him would receive the Spirit. His last breath was the outpouring of the life-giving Spirit.

Father – Son – Spirit: the plenitude of the One God.

The Mystery abides.

Epilogue

At the start of this book we have looked to Genesis. It is fitting, then, to close with a glance at Revelation – Alpha and Omega.

Revelation

Bewilderment – that, in all likelihood, is the reaction of one who comes, for the first time, to the Book of Revelation. Those scrolls and plagues, those elders and living creatures, the dragon and the beasts – what can it possibly be about? Is it any wonder that the book has become a happy-hunting ground for fundamentalists or for those mesmerised by the prospect of the End? Is there any sense to be made of it? In truth, Revelation is a thoroughly Christian writing which, despite first impression, carries a message of startling hope.

One can, however, appreciate why it may disconcert. For, in the first place, it is not easy to classify Revelation. The work is certainly apocalyptic.[1] Yet, its author is, professedly, a prophet, and he writes a letter. Here we leave aside any discussion of the work as a whole and focus on the two figures who dominate Revelation: the Almighty One on the heavenly throne, and the Lamb. The one on the throne displays his power through the Lamb who was slain. In his manner, John, author of Revelation (1:1, 4; 22:8) makes the same point as Paul: 'We proclaim Christ crucified … Christ the power of God and the wisdom of God.' (1 Cor 1:23-24). So fully is the Lamb the manifestation and the very presence of God that, at the end of all, in the New Jerusalem, in place of a temple is a single throne, 'the throne of God and of the Lamb' (Rev 22:1).[2]

God

In Revelation 4:1 John is rapt to heaven. The first object that catches his eye is a throne. He perceives the mysterious presence of One on the throne. That One dominates Revelation. The throne is the symbol of his almighty power. He is Creator and king of creation. He is the Creator who has total respect for his creation. And creation, in its fashion, unceasingly sings his praise (4:8). We know God through human perception of God. That perception will always be culturally conditioned; it will be coloured by the human and historical situation – by circumstances. As a Christian, John saw his God revealed in the Lamb – the Lamb who was slain. That truth coloured his vision of the One on the throne. He would not seek to describe that God, so far beyond any conception of human majesty. Yet, this was no aloof God. He was the God present in the Son. John had been loosed from sin in the blood of that Son (1:5); he had experienced the love of God. Never, for him, could God be a distant God. This awareness, indeed, was not something wholly new. As a Jew, sensitive to the prophetical tradition, he had been familiar with the reality of a transcendent God immersed in the life of his people. The Christ – presence of God – who walks among John's churches (chs 2-3) is playing the role that Yahweh played through his prophets.

'The revelation of Jesus Christ, which God gave him …' (Rev 1:1). God is the ultimate source of Revelation. John bears witness to the secret purpose of God of which Jesus Christ is the prime witness. '"I am the Alpha and the Omega", says the Lord God, who is and who was and who is to come, the Almighty' (1:8). It is the first of only two passages in Revelation where God is explicitly identified as speaker (see 21:5-8). God is 'Almighty', John's favourite title for God. If he is the Almighty, the eternal, sovereign Lord, his might is present in the Lamb (1:4-6). He is ever the foolish God who displays divine power in the cross of Jesus. John's address is full of comfort. We are assured that our God is the everlasting, the Almighty. But we Christians meet this awesome God in the one who laid down his life for us.

The Lamb

The emergence of the Lamb is dramatic even in the setting of this dramatic book. In his vision of the heavenly throne-room (chapter 5), John had been bidden to look out for the Lion of the tribe of Judah. What met his gaze was 'a Lamb standing as though it had been slain' (5:5-6). We ought not be taken by sur-

prise. After all, John's first characterisation of Jesus Christ is as
the one 'who has loosed us from our sins by his blood' (1:5).
Indeed, these words are now caught up in the heavenly canticle:
'… for you were slain and by your blood you bought for God
people from every nation' (5:9). 'Lamb' is John's favourite title
for Christ throughout. We may never overlook that, from the
outset, he is the Lamb who was slain. If John proceeds to paint
the power and triumph of the Lamb, he is clear, and wants it understood, that the decisive victory of the Lamb was won on the
cross.

The 'Wrath' of God

If the sovereignty of God is not in question, the exercise of that
sovereignty does raise questions. There is, on the face of it, an
unsavoury side to the wielding of divine power. One might expect violence from the Dragon (Satan); and there is the prospect
of a persecution of God's people. Instead, violence comes, prin-
cipally, from the One on the throne and from the Lamb! The
'wrath' of God is emphasised, a wrath poured out in a series of
increasingly destructive plagues.

Revelation can easily give an impression of implacable divine wrath – even a strong flavour of vindictiveness. A first step
toward a proper grasp of this aspect of the book might be a consideration of the Genesis flood story. There, too, at first sight,
God is stirred to violent action against sin and sinners. The flood
story is myth, a story of fundamental symbols which are vehi-
cles of ultimate meaning. Myth speaks timeless truth, truth vital
for human existence; it brings out the supernatural dimension of
events. In the flood story we see the holy God's radical incompatibility with sin – God's grief over human sin. The flood is not
an historical event; it is a mythical event. The flood story assures
us that God will have the last word: 'never again shall there be a
flood to destroy the earth' (Gen 9:13). Revelation, too, is myth.
The plagues exist in vision only. The great battle of Armag-
eddon (Rev 19:11-21; see 16:16) is not a historical but a mythical
battle. Nothing of the violence of the plagues is literal violence
against our world; it is violence in visionary scenes of the future,
couched in metaphorical language. Again, just as there is no
'real' flood, there were no 'real' plagues of Egypt, and there

were not, nor will there ever be, 'real' plagues of Revelation. John is convinced of universal human sinfulness (Christians also are sinners [1:5]). The eschatological terrors are the expression of his sense of justice. That is why God and Lamb are the source of violence; Christians can only be victims, not perpetrators, of violence (13:9-10). After all, it is the Lamb, by breaking the first seal, who unleashes the plagues – for all three cycles are interconnected – the Lamb 'who was slain from the foundation of the world'. There is no divine violence against evil.

God is the patient God, but he cannot ignore evil; he will not condone oppression. There is a place for his 'wrath', his radical incompatibility with evil. He copes with evil in his way. His answer to the worst that humankind can perpetrate is the answer of the cross. God is not vindictive. God does not punish. The problem for humans – and it is a humanly insoluble problem – is to maintain faith in the long-suffering of God and, at the same time, to grasp, and find some way to express, his abhorrence of evil and sin. Our human imagination and our human imagery and language are inadequate. Unhappily, we too readily end up by presenting an unsavoury image of our gracious God.

Judgement

At the last judgement scene (20:11-15), John sees 'a great white throne'. Now is the moment for the final word of the One on the throne. The old earth and heaven fade away in radical renewal. Now is the time for the 'new heavens and a new earth, where righteousness is at home' (2 Pet 3:13). In the new world of God, righteousness reigns not only supreme but wholly. There is no place for any shadow of evil.

The dead, 'great and small' – all the dead – stand before the throne of judgement. It is judgement, and 'books were opened': the books which contain a record of the deeds of human beings now come for judgement. But there is 'another book': this book of life is the register of the citizens of the heavenly Jerusalem; it is the book of life of the Lamb. 'Books were opened … the book of life': we are faced with the mystery of salvation. People are judged by their deeds; and yet salvation is free gift (v 15). Our God has created us free and respects our freedom totally. That is why his grace is, so often, thoroughly disguised. We come, later, to discern, in our most painful episodes, his graciousness. Freedom is costly; it exacts the price of responsibility. We are answerable for our deeds – and our omissions. Yet, all the while, our salvation is wholly grace. 'Justified by his grace as a gift, through the redemption that is in Christ Jesus' (Rom 3:24). We are responsible for what we do; we are judged by works. God is author of our salvation; we are saved by grace. John, like the Bible in general, does not attempt to resolve the tension. Later Christian theologians, courageously, stubbornly – and vainly – strove to find a way past the dilemma. The theologians of the Bible, in their wisdom, were content to leave the matter in the hands of God.

New Creation
'Then I saw a new heaven and a new earth; for the first heaven and the first earth had passed away …' (21:1).

John has not dragged in his concept of 'a new heaven and a new earth'. Not alone is the idea thoroughly biblical, but his 'new world' opens up the perspective of an eschatological future in which the cosmos is redeemed and perfected. This is not a restoration of our broken world to its imagined original state, but a transformation beyond imagining, a transformation so radical as to be a 'new creation'. In all of this the human aspect is firmly in mind. Thus, in this new world 'death will be no more; mourning and crying and pain will be no more' (21:4). Paul had already spoken of the redemption of the cosmos in the context of human redemption: the whole of nature shares in the birthpangs which lead to the freedom of the children of God (Rom 8:18-23). The biblical view of the world maintains an intimate link between the cosmos and humankind (Gen 1-2).

This is a matter of first importance. It means that the promise of a new world implies a radical questioning of our present relationship with the world – this world as it was, originally, envisaged by God. It is a reminder that we humans have sinned grievously against God's earth, committed to our care (Gen 1:26-20). We are summoned to *metanoia*, called to work toward the new world held in prospect. True, it is God who declares, 'I make all things new.' But God has freely, from the start, involved humans in his creation. In his plan a new world for humanity can only be with human involvement.

Life With God

'Behold, God's dwelling is with humankind' (21:3). What is eternal life with God? We, in our earthly existence, creatures of time and space, must, perforce, picture heavenly reality in terms of time and space. Here, John has two central images. There will be a new heaven and a new earth. The dragon once had his place in the old heaven; he had ravaged the old earth. A creation that is, at last, utterly free of evil, can only be new. Humankind was the summit of God's creation, divine pride and joy (Gen 1:26-31). God's destined home for humankind was the garden of delights (2:15). There will be a new home for humanity in the new creation: a city, city of God, the New Jerusalem. It is a heavenly city, yet a habitat of men and women.

John surpasses himself in his surrealistic painting of the new Jerusalem. After all, how is one to describe a city of God, a city that is the perfect home of wholly redeemed humankind? It is a city without a temple. God and Lamb reign indeed, but not in the formality of a cultic setting. They dwell in the midst of their people. Our God is never an aloof, distant God – though we tend to make him such. He will be with us always: 'He will dwell among them, and they will be his peoples' (21:3).

God and Lamb

A distinctive feature of John's presentation of the Lamb is his assimilation of the Lamb to God. It is his way of depicting God as the God who has revealed himself in Jesus Christ, who has defined himself in Christ. This conjunction of God and Lamb, as in 5:13 – 'Blessing and honour, glory and might, to the One seated on the throne and to the lamb for ever and ever' – which recurs in 7:10; 21:22; 22:1, 3, represents an advanced christology. The same worship is offered to God and Lamb, just as the throne of both is the same. The multitude of the saved attribute their victory to 'God and the Lamb' (7:10). The heavenly Jerusalem has no temple – 'for its temple was the Lord God Almighty and the Lamb' – and the Lamb is the lamp of the heavenly city (21:22-23). When the throne appears for the last time, now in the city-temple, it is 'the throne of God and of the Lamb' (12:1, 3). Throughout 22:3-4 the pronoun 'his' (his servants, his face, his name) refers to God and Lamb in tandem. Accordingly, the

Lamb can declare of himself: 'I am the Alpha and the Omega, the first and the last, the beginning and the end' (22:13) – echoing the words of the One on the throne (21:6). We might understand the Lamb to speak as does the Johannine Jesus: 'I and the Father are one' (Jn 10:30).

The parallel is instructive. The Johannine Jesus is one with the Father precisely because he is the one sent, the agent of the Father, and is thereby empowered to speak the words of God. John's Lamb is the 'faithful witness' (Rev 1:5) who has received his revelation from God (1:1). It is because of his faithfulness to his witness-bearing, a faithfulness that brought him to the cross, that he shares the throne of God. It is no less clear to the Lamb than it is to the Johannine Jesus that 'the Father is greater than I' (Jn 14:28). The one sent and the faithful witness have this in common. They also share the declaration: 'Whoever has seen me has seen the Father' (14:9). 'I and the father are one'; 'the throne of God and of the Lamb' – these tell us nothing of the 'nature' of the Son/Lamb but tell us everything of the role of Revealer that is the role of the Son/Lamb. For each John, Jesus is the one in whom God is fully present. God is the one who reveals himself wholly in Jesus. But, this God we know in and through Jesus of Nazareth is still, for us, Holy Mystery, veiled in the humanity of the Son. *Ho logos sarx egeneto* – 'the Word became flesh'.

Notes

INTRODUCTION

1. Wilfrid J. Harrington, *The Prodigal Father* (Wilmington, DE: M. Glazier, 1982); *The Tears of God* (Collegeville: Liturgical Press, 1992); *God Does Care* (Dublin/Westminster, MD: Columba Press/Christian Classics, 1994); *Hold On To Hope* (Dublin: Dominican Publications, 1998); *Seeking Spiritual Growth Through The Bible* (New York: Paulist Press, 2002); *From the Presence of the Lord* (Dublin: Columba Press, 2006); *Jesus Our Brother. The Humanity of the Lord* (New York: Paulist Press, 2010).

CHAPTER ONE

1. Elizabeth A. Johnson, *Quest for the Living God* (New York/London: Continuum, 2007) p 15
2. *De potentia*, q. 7, a. 5.
3. Elizabeth A. Johnson, op. cit., p 19.
4. See Ruth Page, *God and the Web of Creation* (London: SCM, 1996).
5. Joan Chittister, 'The God who Beckons', *National Catholic Reporter*, September 4, 2009.

CHAPTER TWO

1. Op. cit., p 64
2. A widely-held corollary of male-oriented God-language is that maleness represents God in a way that femaleness cannot. If this were only theory it would merely be ridiculous. In practice, the attitude has sustained the domination of men and the subordination of women, not only in society at large but tragically in the churches too. Divine transcendence is compromised when it is maintained that God is more appropriately represented as male rather than female. Jesus addressed God as Father – indeed, more intimately, as Abba.

He thereby expressed their relationship in the conventional language of his concrete human state. This tells us not only of his personal relationship with God but the rich meaning of fatherhood in his Hebrew tradition. This aspect has serious theological implications. But the use of the title 'Father', even by Jesus, does not mean that God is, in any sense, male. Appreciation of analogical language reminds us that we do not know what it means for God to be 'Parent'. It surely does not mean that God is male – or female, for that matter. To wield the alleged maleness of God as a weapon of domination is perverse. Macho God is an idol.

3. *Thomasina* (Penguin Books, 1987), p 146.
4. Antoine de Saint-Exupery, *The Little Prince* (Penguin Books, 1962), p 84.
5. *Covenant and Promise* (London: SCM, 1977), p 196.

CHAPTER THREE

1. *Theology of the Old Testament* (Minneapolis: Fortress,1997), p 735. This treatment of justice in the Old Testament is based on Walter Brueggemann's brilliant study.
2. Op. cit., p 738.
3. Abraham Heschel, *The Prophets*, Vol II (New York: Harper and Roe, 1962), 'The Theology of Pathos', pp 285-297; 'The Meaning and Mystery of Wrath', pp 358-381. This is the classic study.
4. Op. cit.
5. Terence E. Fretheim, *The Suffering of God* (Philadelphia: Fortress Press, 1984), p 12.

CHAPTER FOUR

1. Wilfrid J. Harrington, *From the Presence of the Lord. A God too Gracious* (Dublin: the Columba Press, 2006), pp 27-38; See Paul Murray, *A Journey With Jonah. The Spirituality of Bewilderment* (Dublin: The Columba Press, 2002).
2. *For the Sake of the Gospel* (New York: Crossword, 1990), p 93.
3. Bruce, C. Birch, *et al*, *A Theological Introduction to the Old Testament* (Nashville: Abingdon press, 1999), p 55.
4. Baruch 1:15-3:8; Ezra 9:6-18; Nehemiah 1:5-11; 9:6-37; Tobit 13:1-8; Sirach 36:1-17; Esther 13:9-17; 14:3-19; Judith 9:2-14; Daniel 3:26-45; 9:4-19.

5. Wilfrid J. Harrington, *Hold on to Hope* (Dublin: Dominican Publications, 1998), pp 15-35. An Appendix (pp 83-86) gives a list of the occurrences of the feature of abrupt fluctuation of judgement and salvation throughout the prophetical literature. It graphically illustrates the pervasiveness of this remarkable contrast.

6. *Jesus in Our Western Culture* (London: SCM, 1987), p 8.

7. 'The most serious heresy of European Christianity, especially in the last few centuries, has been the reduction of the gospel to little more than the salvation of souls. I make bold to call it a heresy. Technically I suppose I would have to say that it was a material heresy rather than a formal heresy because it was not deliberate. European Christians, as far as one knows, did not choose to go into heresy. They simply drifted into it. Perhaps some of them could be accused of culpable ignorance. I don't know and at this stage it doesn't really matter.' *God in South Africa. The Challenge of the Gospel* (Grand Rapids: Eerdmans, 1988), pp 108-109.

8. Edward Schillebeeckx, ibid., p 7.

9. See Wilfrid J. Harrington, op. cit., pp 59-64.

10. Paul Achtemeier has put it finely: 'From the stuff of human disobedience, God has shaped the means of his mercy' (v 32). That is the conclusion to which Paul comes in this passage [11:25-36] … Mercy is God's response to disobedient Israel as it is his response to disobedient gentiles … If it seems a strange way to go about the redemption of creation … it is a striking example of the omnipotence of God.' *Romans* (Atlanta: John Knox Press, 1985), p 187.

11. 'The "eschaton" or the ultimate is exclusively positive. There is no negative eschaton. Good, not evil, has the last word.' Edward Schillebeeckx, *Church: The Human Story of God* (London: SCM, 1999), p 136.

CHAPTER FIVE

1. *The Epistle of Paul to the Romans* (London: Collins, 1959), p 55.

2. In discussing what he terms 'forgotten truths' about penance, Sean Fagan observes: 'Perhaps the greatest and most forgotten truth of all is that God's forgiveness is sheer gift, unearned, unmerited. In our concern to see that God is

not mocked or even slighted, we may have lost our perspective. Though we speak of the gift of his forgiveness, most people feel that they must earn it, be worthy of it, that it comes only after they have done their penance, paid their fine. But this is not the impression we get from Jesus. Both in his own ministry of forgiveness and in his preaching, he makes it clear that the initiative comes from God, that forgiveness is the gift of his love and that the works of penance are the result of it, not the condition of its granting.' *What Happened to Sin?* (Dublin: The Columba Press, 2008), p 190.

Herbert McCabe puts it even more forthrightly: 'Never be deluded into thinking that if you have contrition, if you are sorry for your sins, God will come and forgive you – that he will be touched by your appeal, change his mind about you and forgive you. Not a bit of it. God never changes his mind about you. He is simply in love with you. What he does, again and again, is change your mind about him. That is why you are sorry. That is what your forgiveness is. You are not forgiven because you confess your sin. You confess your sin, recognise yourself for what you are, because you are forgiven.' *Faith Within Reason* (London: Continuum, 2007).

CHAPTER SIX

1. Edward Schillebeeckx, *Jesus in our Western Culture* (London: SCM, 1987), p 28.
2. Op. cit., pp 19-20.
3). Because the matter is so important it seems helpful to list some key texts which underline the perversity of the accepted satisfaction theory.

'If while we were enemies we were reconciled to God by the death of his Son, much more, now that we are reconciled, shall we be saved by his life.' (Rom 5:10). 'He who did not spare his own Son but gave him up for us all, will he not also give us all things with him?' (8:32). 'For God so loved the world that he gave his only Son, that whoever believes in him should not perish but have eternal life. For God sent the Son into the world, not to condemn the world, but that the world might be saved through him' (Jn 3:16-17). 'My little children, I am writing these things to you so that you may not sin. But if anyone does sin, we have an advocate (*parakletos*) with the Father, Jesus Christ the righteous; and he is the expiation for our sins, and not for ours only but also for the sins of the whole world' (1 Jn 2:1-2). 'God is love. In this the love of God was made manifest among us, that God sent his only Son into the world, so that we might live through him. In this is love, not that we loved God but that he loved us and sent his Son to be the expiation for our sins' (4:8-9). The same purpose is implicitly present in the High Priest christology of Hebrews (2:17-18; 4:14-16; 5:7-10; 7:25). The truth is: theories of propitiation and satisfaction can stand only if such texts are overlooked – indeed only if the whole New Testament is ignored.

4. Lisa Sowle Cahill, 'Salvation and the Cross', *Concilium*.

5. 'On the cross Jesus shared in the brokenness of our world. This means that God determines in absolute freedom, down the ages, who and how he wills to be in his deepest being, namely a God of men and women, an ally in our suffering and our absurdity and also an ally in the good that we do. In his own being he is a God for us. I therefore can no longer see any significance to the classic difference between "God in himself" and "God for us".'

   In the New Testament there is a theological redefinition of various concepts of God, and also a redefinition of what it means to be human. God accepts men and women unconditionally, and precisely through this unconditional acceptance he transforms them and calls them to repentance and renewal. Therefore the cross is also a judgement on our own views: a judgement on our ways of living out the meaning of being human and being God. Here is revealed ultimately and definitively the kingdom of God: God who comes into his own in the world of human beings for their healing and happiness, even through suffering.' Edward Schillebeeckx, *Church. The Human Story of God* (London: SCM, 1990), p 126.

6. *Jesus Before Christianity* (New York: Orbis Books, 1978), pp 136-137.

EPILOGUE

1. 'Apocalypse', from the Greek *apocalypsis* ('revelation') designates a type of Jewish literature which flourished from about
   200 BCE to 100 CE. As a literary form it is presented as a revelation, or series of revelations, of heavenly secrets made to a
   seer and conveyed in highly symbolic imagery. It is a crisis
   literature. The biblical apocalypses are the book of Daniel
   (more precisely, Dan 7-12), and the Revelation of John.
   Apocalypticism is the worldview of an apocalyptic movement. In this view it is taken for granted that a supernatural
   world stands above our earthly world. That heavenly world
   is the 'real' world. There is a twofold dualism: vertical, the
   world above and our world, and horizontal, our age and the
   age to come. There is always a definitive eschatological
   judgement: the final clash between good and evil, issuing in
   the total victory of God and the end of evil. Apocalyptic
   ideas pervade the New Testament.
2. Wilfrid J. Harrington, *Revelation,* Sacra Pagina 16, (Collegeville:
   Liturgical Press, 1993); *Revelation: Proclaiming a Vision of Hope*
   (San Jose: Resource Publications, 1994).